EAST MEETS WEST

A Bridge to Understanding, Friendship, Trust, Peace and Prosperity
Between my Mother and Adopted Countries

EAST MEETS WEST

A Bridge to Understanding, Friendship, Trust, Peace and Prosperity
Between my Mother and Adopted Countries

© 2017

ISBN: 978-0-692-79716-7

Text: Mae Yih
Book Design: Reynolds Wulf Inc.
Production: RLO Media Productions
Prepress: Mars Premedia
Printed and bound in China

EAST MEETS WEST

A Bridge to Understanding, Friendship, Trust, Peace and Prosperity
Between my Mother and Adopted Countries

By Mae Yih

*Explaining to my colleagues why I should be elected
as President of the Oregon State Senate on January 11, 1993.*

This book is dedicated to the individuals
who have played an important role in my life:

To my father, who taught me the importance
of hard work, discipline, thrift, and education;

To my mother, who also stressed the value of a good education,
and who instilled in me an appreciation
of modern and ancient Chinese calligraphy and art;

To my husband, Stephen, for his love, encouragement,
faith in my ability, and strong support for my service
on school boards and the state legislature;

To Barnard College President Millicent McIntosh,
for her weekly speeches urging students to use their education
and be involved in their community for the benefit of the community.

To Roger Reid, who chaired all my state legislative campaigns,
and who provided constant and astute advice that was
key to the success of those campaigns;

To Jeanne Dost who co-chaired many of initial legislative campaigns,
and who provided special help to understanding issues, meeting people,
and attending events in the Benton County area, where I was less known.

To my colleagues on school boards and the Oregon State Legislature;
my legislative staff; the volunteers who worked on my campaigns;
and all the constituents in my House and Senate districts:
I thank you for the friendship you extended me,
and the trust you placed in me.

*Finally, I dedicate this book to the memory of Stephen's
great-grandfather, Ye Cheng Zhong,*
whose high integrity and honesty helped him to achieve
success in business far above his humble beginnings
as a sampan ferry rowboat man.

Dear Grandsons Stephen, Alex, Christopher and Benjamin:

As I look back on my life, it is clear that I have been very fortunate. I was blessed to have a father and a mother who instilled values that have always guided me. Because of their efforts, I was able to come to America and receive an education from an outstanding college. I had 56 years of marriage to a loving, generous, and hard-working husband with high integrity and compassion for his family, colleagues, employees and community. (You can learn more the high moral principles and hard work of grandfather Stephen and great-great grandfather Ye Cheng Zhong in the Stephen Yih biography I wrote and published and gave to you in 2011). Together, we raised two intelligent, healthy and successful sons—a cardiologist practicing in Philadelphia, and an attorney turned business executive in Connecticut.

Through volunteer involvement in schools, and service on school boards and in the Oregon State Legislature, and in spite of the fact that I lived in a state where the Chinese-American population was less than 0.5%, I was able to be elected and give back to my community, my state and my mother and adopted countries. My involvement in the community and my service in the legislature also gave me the opportunity to visit the White House; to testify before the United States Congress; to campaign for and meet President John F. Kennedy, to meet President Ronald Reagan, President George H.W. Bush, President Bill Clinton, and Vice President Al Gore, and to also meet with a number of leaders of China, including Premiers Deng Xiao Ping, Zhao Xi Yang, Zhu Yong Ji, Jiang Xi Ming, and Vice Premier Wen Jia Pao.

My public service career also led the two biggest newspapers in my legislative district, the Albany Democrat Herald and the Corvallis Gazette Times, to name me in 1999 as one of the region's "outstanding leaders of the 20th century." Above all, I am pleased with the small positive difference I made in improving the quality of life of the citizens I represented and by acting as a bridge to improve understanding, friendship, trust, peace and prosperity between my beloved adopted country and my mother country.

Because I live in Oregon and the four of you were born and raised on the east coast, one of the regrets of my life is that I have not been able to see you as much as I would have liked. Your grandfather was sorry about this, too. He and I often talked about how proud we were of you and your fathers, how we wished we could spend more time with you, and we wondered what your future would hold.

I have thought a lot about your future, and how I might be able to help ensure that it is a bright one. Your lives are busy with work or school or friends, and it will only get busier in the years ahead. The last thing you want is your grandmother calling up on a daily basis with words of wisdom and advice. But I do believe that some of the experiences and lessons from my life's journey might be helpful to you. So I sat down at my computer (a newly acquired skill!) and began to write you a letter sharing those experiences and lessons. As you can see, it became a very long letter!

It is my hope that in the years to come, you will read and re-read this letter. I believe you will be a much richer and fuller person if you do. I also hope that eventually each of you will have a family, and that you will share this letter with them so they can learn more about their great grandmother and great grandfather and those who came before us.

Mae Yih
December, 2016

My brother Tom and I pose with our mother in 1932.

Let me begin my story by sharing the most important lesson of all.

And that's the fact that there is nothing more important than family. Everything I achieved in life was only achieved because of the love and support and sacrifice of my parents and my family. I know the same will be true for you.

I was born on May 24, 1928, the "Year of the Dragon," in Shanghai, China, where I would spend the first 19 years of my life. My father was Chun Woo Dunn, and my mother was Fung Wen Feng Dunn. They both were remarkable individuals. My mother's name means a "beautiful phoenix," and my Chinese name is Chih Feng Dunn, which means "little phoenix."

My father was an astute, self-made millionaire. He came from a very poor family in the city of Jiang Ying, which is approximately 125 miles west of Shanghai. He was raised by his mother, as his father died when he was very young. Because his family could not afford his schooling beyond grade school, he was sent at a young age to work as an apprentice for a shop owner in Shanghai. Father realized very quickly during his apprenticeship that you had to be able to speak English in order to conduct any business in Shanghai, a large metropolitan city at the eastern coast of China. Every night after work, around midnight, he studied the English dictionary under candlelight and taught himself enough English to be able to conduct business transactions. Due to his diligence and intelligence, his boss eventually gave him a promotion and asked him to be a sales-man, specializing in cotton goods.

In 1922, when he was only eighteen years of age, my father decided that he wanted to start his own business. He managed to scrimp and borrow $500 to establish his own company. He soon decided instead of selling flour sacks as a middleman, he should manufacture his own cotton goods. In 1931 he built his own cotton manufacturing plant, which included a knitting yarn manufacturing division. He was innovative, frugal, and worked around the clock to make his business succeed. His "Hero" brand knitting yarn competed successfully with the better known British "Honey Bee" brand due to his careful research into the right texture, most popular colors, and affordable prices. (I was a good customer as I was taught to knit and embroider when I was five years old!)

My father also made time to attend law classes in the evenings, so he could defend himself in the case of lawsuits. By 1948, he was ranked as the fourth wealthiest man in Shanghai, and he was the sole owner of six enterprises: three mills—one of which was the first rayon manufacturing plant in China— a prestigious 200-room hotel at the "Bund," a premier international business district bordering the harbor, a popular nightclub, an automobile and motorcycle dealership, and a business that imported and exported raw material and equipment. He was acclaimed as the "father of man-made synthetic fiber-rayon manufacturing in China."

My mother was born in Hong Kong, and was a very talented calligrapher, a classical art taught to her by her father. As a young woman, she gave exhibitions of her large ancient style calligraphy, and met my father when he came to an exhibition she gave in Shanghai in hopes of buying a new custom designed sign for his company. A romance blossomed, and marriage soon followed.

Father and Mother would have three children together—I arrived between my older brother, Tom, and my younger brother, Jim. There were, however, other members of our household. Father had another son and daughter before he married my mother. Their names were Jack and Ying. They came to live with us when they were 11 and 13 years of age. Sadly, Ying would pass away from acute tuberculosis two years later.

Chinese culture in the early part of the 20th century was very different than it is today. Then, it was common practice for wealthy and successful men to have official "concubines"—women they supported as a spouse, provided housing for, and often fathered children with. Father had three concubines and an additional six children! It's hard for people today to imagine, but my brothers and I were all on cordial terms with my father's concubines (or "Aunts" as we called them) and our six half-brothers and sisters.

Needless to say, with one wife, three concubines, four households, ten children, and a very successful business enterprise, my father's schedule was incredibly busy. He devised a rotation system where he would live in each of his households for two consecutive days before moving on to the next. Sundays were often a time for father to bring all his families together for a lunch at a fancy restaurant and an afternoon of folk opera performance.

One thing my brothers and I never doubted, however, was that our father loved us very much. When he was home, he would spend as much time with us as possible. He didn't want to waste a minute, and even when he was on the toilet in the morning, he would call my brothers and I to listen to his stories of his days as a struggling apprentice who had to attend to all chores of the shop as well as personal chores for the owner and his wife, including cleaning their night commodes every morning. Father usually cried when he talked about his apprenticeship days. He would also ask us to recite our multiplication charts, telling us that the charts were extremely important to remember in order to facilitate the use of the abacus, which was used in every business office at that time. (Many years later, I would bring my abacus to use as a calculator to my first meeting as a Clover Ridge School Board member—much to the surprise of my fellow board members!)

The fact that Father was gone so frequently also meant that when he came home he often spoiled us with fancy pastries, delicacies of the season and frequent gifts. During the fall, when large freshwater lake crabs were in season, he would bring home strings of live crabs, tied neatly five or six in a string, and treat us to a wonderful feast. He also taught us how to eat the crab neatly, so that by the time we were done eating them, we could still put the shells back together in the shape of a crab.

Our household also included a great deal of pets. Along with a beautiful St. Bernard dog named "Buddha," which my father brought back from Switzerland after a European business trip, our backyard also included monkeys, turkeys, chickens, geese, ducks, goats, pigeons, and a cockatoo who loved to dance and sing. My favorite members of our menagerie, however, were our three horses. My dad loved to take my brothers and I horseback riding on Sunday mornings, and we would take our horses and others we would rent from a nearby stable out for gallops. At least my father and brothers would have horses that galloped—father usually made me ride a very old horse that didn't run very fast!

My father's wealth and success meant that we also had many servants in the house. These included a full time and a part time gardener, three maids, two seamstresses (who could make a dress for my mother or me in a day), one chauffeur, one bodyguard, and two chefs—one for Chinese food and one for western style food. Western food was cooked in a small upstairs kitchen, which had a modern western electric range, oven and toaster. The Chinese meals were prepared in the downstairs main kitchen, and were cooked in large woks that were heated in fires using chopped wood as fuel. I confess that I rarely entered the kitchen, as there was never any need to. In fact, the only time I remember being in the kitchen was during the last two months before I departed for America, when I was nineteen years old. I was advised to learn how to cook because Americans did their own cooking. I watched the chefs a few times—it didn't help, as you can't learn how to cook by watching. Cooking is definitely not my strong point!

Looking back, I know that I was very spoiled as a child. In the summer, whenever I wanted a glass of water, I walked to the landing of the staircase where it led to the western kitchen and to the servants' quarters. I would yell for a glass of cold boiled water and one of the maids would quickly run it to me. I could have walked the few steps it would have taken to get my own glass of water, but the thought never crossed my mind.

The most important benefit that my father's success provided to my brothers and me was a good education. Not only did we go to the finest private schools, we also had tutors come to our home after school to help us with the heavy amount of daily home-work our teachers had assigned us. I also have fond memories of morning sessions of Tai-Chi, a Chinese martial art which is practiced for both self-defense and health benefits. Our instructors were old masters who constantly exercised their fingers by holding and manipulating two walnuts. After years and years of use, these walnuts would eventually turn translucent and purple.

One of my favorite and most enduring memories of my childhood was Chinese New Year—a 15-day holiday of sweets, new clothes, lanterns, "lucky money," fire crackers, and "kow tows," which were New Years greetings to grandparents and parents.

The celebration began the night before New Year's Eve, when, according to tradition, the house had to be thoroughly cleaned and swept. This meant all the "old" was swept away and the house was ready to welcome the "new." Businesses customarily paid all their old debt at this time and started their accounts with a clean slate. We would always have a big family dinner on New Year's Eve featuring many courses of delicious dishes. The morning of New Year's Day, we would be woken up by loud firecrackers, which were meant to chase away evil spirits. Then my brothers and I quickly dress in our finest new clothes and hurry to greet our parents to wish them a Happy New Year. We would kowtow to them and yell "Kung He Fat Choy!" ("Happiness and great prosperity for the New Year!").

They would tell us that we were good children and give us their blessings and red envelopes that contained "lucky money." We then would go give similar greetings to our paternal grandmother, and she, too, would smile and give us a red envelope with money. Many relatives would come visit during the course of the day, and they also would give us lucky money. Unfortunately for us, my mother would usually collect all the red envelopes and money that were given to us, and she would put the money in different envelopes and give them back to relatives for their children. We ended up only getting what our parents and grandmother gave us! The celebration usually ended by January 15, which was the day of the lantern festival. Children would go around in the evening in the courtyard with fancy lanterns. During one celebration that occurred at the peak of my father's prosperity in business, he gave each of us a solid ounce of gold in the shape of yuan bao (the symbol of money) as lucky money. I gave it to my mother to hold in her safety box for me. It is a shame I didn't bring it with me when I came to the United States.

Many families allowed their children to engage in gambling with their holiday lucky money, but my mother forbid children gambling in our household. We weren't even allowed to play mahjong, the tile game that has long been popular in China. Even though she regularly played the game at social gatherings with her friends, she considered it a bad habit and a waste of time. My friends were always surprised when I told them that I didn't know how to play mahjong and wasn't allowed to play the game.

One of the most interesting aspects of my childhood is that much of it was spent in the midst of two wars—the war between Japan and China and World War II—and a dictatorship under Chiang Kai-Shek. Japan invaded China in 1937, and the two countries would remain at war until Japan surrendered in 1945. Shanghai, however, was one of the first battlefields of the war, and the Japanese army occupied and controlled a large portion of Shanghai from 1937-1945. The occupying Japanese soldiers were extremely brutal and were known to use the bayonets on the end of their rifles to stab the stomachs of Chinese farmers, workers, and others who did not bow to them. An area known as the "international settlement," occupied by citizens of neutral countries like the United States, Britain and France, remained relatively independent until the attack on Pearl Harbor in 1941.

There was a massive shortage of goods and rampant inflation during the Japanese occupation and World War II. Even well-to-do families like ours had difficulty in finding or buying everyday items. As a result, we recycled as much and as far as possible. Runs in nylon stockings were mended, worn light bulbs were repaired, pencil stubs were extended, and we wrote on both sides of the paper all the way to the corners. Old habits die hard, and even to this day, I don't throw away nylon stockings, as they can be crocheted into area rugs.

Near the end of World War II, the rule of law completely broke down, and there was constant kidnapping of children of wealthy families. One morning, as Tom, Jack, Jim and I were being driven to school by our chauffeur, three men with machine guns stopped our car. The chauffeur, Jack, Jim and I were ordered out of the car, and the kidnappers drove off with Tom. The kidnappers would subsequently contact my father, and, after a huge ransom was paid, Tom was returned home. He told us of being kept in a closet for days while the ransom negotiations went on. He also came home full of lice, and had to take several baths to get clean. After the kidnapping, we were all sent to live in the dormitory of our schools, and my father hired a Russian bodyguard to go everywhere with us. Shanghai was home to a large population of members of the Russian royal family who had fled there as refugees after the Communists took control in the Russian revolution. In fact, my horseback riding teacher was a former Russian colonel!

My father's success provided us with a very privileged lifestyle in a country where the vast majority of the people were very poor. After World War II ended and the Japanese armies departed Shanghai, China dissolved into civil war. On one side were the forces of the dictator Chang Kai-Shek, who had ruled China since 1928. On the other side were the communist forces of Mao Ze Dong. With a very small number of extremely wealthy citizens, almost no middle class, and an overwhelming number of people living in poverty, China was fertile ground for revolution. People in the countryside were living in mud huts with straw rooftops, and fuel was often supplied by horse or cow manure patties that had been baked in the sun along the sidewalks. In the city, there were beggars on every block and prostitutes on every street corner. In short, the government was riddled with greed, corruption, high taxes, a ruined currency, terrible waste of life, and callous disregard of the welfare of citizens. People were more concerned with bare basic survival than they were with losing their personal freedoms. After the war, as Tom and I were driven in the morning by our chauffeur to the university for our classes, we saw corpses wrapped in straw mats strewn along the roadside. The bodies were those of the homeless or those with families who could not afford a burial. When we came back from school in the mid-afternoon, the roads were cleaner, as the corpses had been removed by the sanitation department trucks.

It is important to remember that while America has many problems, there is no other country on earth that provides its citizens with more freedom and more opportunities than the United States. Certainly, the most important events in my life was my coming to the United States. If I had not done so, I would have likely spent my entire life in a country that denied even the most basic freedoms to its citizens.

Even though it was nearly seventy years ago, I can remember January 24, 1948— the day I left China for the United States—like it was yesterday. Father had sent my brothers Tom and Jim to the United States six months earlier. He wanted them to work with him in his business, and thought it was important for them to learn how to manufacture rayon. The best rayon manufacturing company was in New York City, and an executive of that company who knew my father said he would be happy to provide Tom and Jim an internship, but recommended that after they arrived in New York, they first study chemistry at his alma mater—Princeton University in New Jersey.

Mother decided that she would like to travel to the United States so she could visit Tom and Jim, and to address some medical issues she was experiencing. She wanted me to accompany her to act as her interpreter, as she did not speak English very well at all. Thanks to nine years of English classes in elementary school, high school and college, I was fluent in English. Joining us was "Aunt Number Two," one of my father's concubines, whom Mother had convinced to come with us, as she also had some medical issues. We traveled to America on the maiden voyage of the luxury ocean liner, the "President Cleveland," which was over 600 feet in length and housed 800 passengers. (It also housed our luggage—and we brought quite a lot! Not knowing how long I would be staying, I brought with me 100 "jipaos" (Chinese dresses) suitable for all seasons, so I wouldn't have to worry about running out of dresses in New York. However, all my dresses were about knee length, which was the fashion of the time, and the fashion changed the next year to floor length dresses, so all of mine were out of style, and I had to write home to ask for more to be sent!

The ship made two stops as we sailed across the Pacific. I was very seasick for the first two days but followed advice to walk on deck and breathe fresh sea air, and quickly recovered. Our first stop after leaving China was Japan, where we docked in Tokyo and were given time to go ashore for a few hours. It was a shocking sight. American airplanes had dropped many bombs on Tokyo during the final years of World War II, and there were still many buildings that remained heavily damaged and without roofs. After several more days, we stopped in Honolulu, Hawaii, where the entire crew on the ship changed to crisp white summer uniforms. We were also given a few hours to sight see the beautiful island. Finally, on February 7, 1948 we arrived in San Francisco, California.

The most important event that happened during our two-week voyage was the fact that an American gentleman who knew my father was also on the ship, and he frequently sat at our table during meals. He was a graduate of Columbia University in New York City, and he recommended that while I was in New York, I should attend Barnard College, the all-women school that was affiliated with Columbia.

When we arrived in San Francisco, the customs officer asked me three questions before we were allowed to go ashore.

The first was "Are you returning to China after visiting your brothers in New York City?"

"Of course," I responded.

The second question was "Are you going to get married in America?"

"Of course not," I said. "My father will pick me a good husband when I return to China."

The third and final question was "Are you going to become an American citizen?"

"Of course not!" was my response. "I am returning to China to become my father's personal accountant."

All of my answers were exactly what the customs officer wanted to hear. They were also what I believed and what I intended. They all turned out to be 100% wrong!

After spending a couple of days sightseeing in San Francisco we flew on a commercial airliner to New York City. This was before modern day jets, and the planes were much slower than they are today. The flight took eight hours, was quite bumpy, and I got very airsick.

When we arrived in New York, my brother, Tom, had made arrangements for us to stay in a hotel near Times Square and close to the rayon manufacturing company. I immediately followed up on the shipboard advice made by father's business associate, whom I called "Uncle Emile." (In China, all friends of parents are either called "Uncle" or "Aunt" as a sign of respect.) Uncle Emile had advised me to apply for admission to Barnard. While they were very interested in adding foreign students to their student population, I had missed the registration deadline for the semester, and they invited me to enroll that fall. In the meantime, they suggested I apply to Hunter College, a city college in New York City. I did just that, and was soon enrolled in Economics and typing classes.

The next several months were busy ones as I completed my courses at Hunter, and Mother, Aunt Number Two, and I moved into an apartment on the east side of Manhattan that came with an Irish maid for cooking and housekeeping. While I was becoming accustomed to the freedom of living in the United States, which included navigating New York City's subway and bus system, my father's situation was deteriorating. The long civil war between the government forces of Chiang Kai-shek and the Communist forces led by Mao Ze Dong was nearing the end, as the Communists took control of Shanghai.

As a prominent businessman, my father was considered as a capitalist who was guilty of exploitation of labor. As such, he was placed under arrest and jailed. He would not be let out of jail until five years later, and I would not see him again until 1974—twenty-six years after I left China.

Some 46 years after I left China—in May of 1994— I spoke to the first annual Asian/Pacific Islander American Celebration Week at Oregon State University. I took the opportunity to share with the audience how I learned to serve the people of my district from my Confucian studies in Shanghai. I attributed my success as a public servant to the constant teaching in school and at home of the importance of strong ethics and high moral standards. It was these teachings that helped me to insist on doing what is right, and that gave me strength and confidence. It was my experience in my schooling in China during the war, when we only had half-day school with another half a day of homework, that convinced me that good education does not need to be expensive. It is the quality of the curriculum and hard work of the students and teachers that make the difference.

In my speech, I shared a story that I learned during history lessons in high school. It was a story about a well-known Chinese general by the name of Chang Lien. He was renowned for his strategies in war. When he was a young student, he walked behind a crippled old man who dropped his shoe as he crossed a bridge. Chang picked up his shoe and the old man asked him to put it on for him. Chang did this, and then the old man dropped his shoe again and again. Each time, young Chang patiently picked it up and put it on the old man's foot. Finally, the old man looked at Chang and said, "Come here tomorrow morning at dawn and I will have a book of great learning for you."

When Chang arrived the next morning at dawn, the old man was already there. "You are too late," he said to Chang. "Come back tomorrow at dawn, and I will have a book for you." The next morning, Chang got up earlier, and ran to the bridge at the crack of dawn. Again, the old man was already there, and again, he told Chang that he was too late and to come back the next morning.

The next morning, Chang arrived at the bridge before dawn, and waited for the old man to come. When the old man arrived, he gave Chang a book of the strategies of war and told him that the book could only be given to a student of humility, patience and persistence. Chang had proven to him that he had those qualities. Young Chang studied hard and went on to become one of the best-known generals in Chinese history.

The importance of humility, patience, and persistence was also a lesson learned from my father's life. He liked to quote the saying, "It is only when you have endured the bitterest of the bitter that you can become the highest of the high."

CHAPTER 2: **My New Life in America**

In the fall of 1948, I officially enrolled in Barnard as a sophomore Economics major, moved into a dormitory, and began what was to be a very eventful and memorable period. My mother and Aunt Number Two had hoped that I would live with them while attending Barnard, but living in the dorm gave me more time to study and to be involved in school activities. I told Mother that any time she needed me, I was only thirty minutes away by subway and bus.

My years at Barnard College were full of friends and many wonderful memories. Some of the most vivid of these were the student assemblies held at the beginning of each academic year. All 800 or so students would gather for a series of speeches from university officials—including one from the President of Columbia University, Dwight D. Eisenhower. Eisenhower was probably the most famous and respected man in the world at that time, having accepted the Presidency of Columbia after serving as Supreme Commander of the Allied Forces in World War II. He would, by popular demand, go on to be elected President of the United States in 1952 and 1956. Every time he came to speak to Barnard students, we would cheer and yell and whoop it up, as we were always excited to see this true hero. Eisenhower's face would light up with his famous broad smile, and he would say, "In front of thousands of soldiers, I am relaxed. But in front of 800 young women, I am nervous and speechless." That would cause the students to cheer and scream some more.

Eisenhower also played an important role in my receiving a college education. After the Communist revolution in China, many Chinese students were stranded in America without being able to receive financial support from their families in China. Eisenhower did not want to see nuclear science students forced to return to China, so he established scholarship funds to pay tuition and to provide living expenses for science students. The program was soon expanded to include liberal arts students like me. Without this scholarship I would not have been able to afford to continue at Barnard and would not have graduated.

One of the graduation requirements at Barnard was that every student be able to speak two foreign languages. Since Chinese was my native language, it did not count as a foreign language, but English did. I then took a year of French to satisfy the requirement. I mention this because the ability to understand multiple languages is even more important in today's global marketplace. In addition, when you study a foreign language you also learn more about your own language. As an example, when I studied the complicated grammar of French, I learned more about English grammar at the same time.

I learned many lessons during my years at Barnard, but the most important of them wasn't learned in the classroom. Rather, it was learned in a student assembly. Millicent

McIntosh was the Dean and then President of Barnard from 1947 until 1962. She was a wise, warm, and gracious woman who challenged Barnard students to live a full and contributing life. At a time when women were still not granted the same rights as men, President McIntosh foresaw a time when women would not have any door closed to them. She would share important remarks at our weekly student assembly, and invariably she would repeat the message— "Use your education, be involved in the decision making process for the benefit of your community." Those words would have a profound impact on my life, as they were the words that would later inspire me to begin the journey that would lead to my public service career. (I was able to pay tribute to President McIntosh in 2011, when I attended my 60th Barnard class reunion. I was invited to give a brief talk with six other alumnae, and I focused my remarks on the tremendous influence that she had on my life.)

There was another very important event in my life that occurred during my time at Barnard—I met Stephen Yih. Like most Chinese students, he lived near the Columbia campus, and often came to tea dances at Barnard. However, he did not date me until two years later, after he received his Masters degree and got a job. Believe it or not, he asked me to marry him on our very first date! I didn't say "yes" then, but it didn't take me long to realize that he was a thoughtful and sincere man with whom I wanted to spend the rest of my life.

Stephen and I were married on June 7, 1953. I had received my undergraduate degree from Barnard, completing three years of classes in two-and-a-half years, had taken a year of graduate courses in accounting at the Columbia University Graduate School of Business, and was working in the finance office at Barnard. Stephen had received master's degrees in electrical engineering from Brooklyn Polytechnical Institute, and in mechanical engineering from New York University, and was working for Wah Chang, a tungsten manufacturing and trading firm in New York.

Our first years of married life in an apartment on Long Island were busy and frugal ones. Stephen made $600 a month as an engineer, and I made $200 a month at Barnard— $100 of which I gave to my mother to help with her expenses, and $30 I sent to my half-sister Christine who had been able to leave Communist China for Hong Kong.

Our family grew on September 20, 1954 when Donald was born. Because Stephen was too nervous to drive me to the hospital, we were driven by his brother, David, who had come to America from China to attend graduate school at Stephen's invitation and sponsorship. David lived us with for two years, while Stephen coached him in the evenings in his graduate studies at NYU in Aeronautical Engineering.

Stephen was a very proud dad. Nowadays, it is common for fathers to be very involved in caring for their children. Back in the 1950's, that wasn't the case. Stephen was unique among his friends in that he would insist on getting up at 2:00 in the morning to feed Donald, even though he had to get up a few hours later to go to work.

In June of 1955, Steve came home to tell me that his employer, Wah Chang Corporation, had transferred him to Boulder City, Nevada to work on titanium research at the U. S. Bureau of Mines facility there. I asked him why he had been selected for this assignment, and he said that he had volunteered to make the move. Why was he the only engineer who volunteered to move across country to work on a new project on which he had no experience? It was because he saw it as a chance to learn, advance, excel, and to prove himself to his boss. And that is exactly what he did.

While in Nevada, Steve would be successful in improving the quality of titanium, and in 1956 Steve was asked to accept an assignment in Albany, Oregon. It was in Albany, of course, where Steve would earn a reputation as one of the most brilliant and visionary leaders in the metals industry, where we would spend our life and make our home, where our second son, Daniel, would join our family in April 1958, and where I would enter the public service arena. I have often thought how different our life might have been had Steve not volunteered to go to Nevada. Perhaps we never would have ended up in Oregon. It all happened because Steve had the courage and the guts to take a risk.

For two people who had spent all their lives in large urban areas, living in the rural area of Linn County and Albany was quite an adventure at first. I remember one evening soon after we arrived in Albany where we lived in a rental house in the countryside. I looked outside and saw a cute baby animal on our patio. The animal had a bushy black tail with a white silvery stripe in the middle of its back and it looked like a little kitten. I asked Steve to catch it with a laundry basket and bring it inside to see if perhaps it would play with Donald, and we were shocked by a very sharp and pungent smell, which immediately shot in the air. I ran around the house screaming and opening all the windows! It took at least three days for the terrible smell to go away. As I'm sure you have figured out, the animal wasn't a kitten—it was a skunk! When Steve told this story to his colleagues in his company, no one expressed any sympathy. All they did was laugh! In our defense, there were no skunks in Shanghai, China or New York City, and Steve and I had never seen one before in our whole lives!

We also raised 35 baby chicks to roosters without intending to do so. On one Easter morning, I asked Steve to buy a couple of baby chicks for Donald. Steve said they were three cents each. Not to appear cheap, he bought one-dollar worth of chicks from a farmer, who then threw in two extra chicks for good measure. I didn't know what to do with them, so I raised them in the bathroom. Pretty soon, they outgrew the bathroom, so we quickly built a chicken coop for them. Thanks to all the good chicken feed, the 35 cute baby chicks became 35 full grown roosters that crowed loudly every morning and often chased two-year-old Donald, pecking him every chance they had. We soon decided it was time to get rid of them, but Steve couldn't even catch one to take it to the slaughterhouse. We finally consulted with our farmer neighbor who advised us that at dusk, the roosters were all perching on the fence, where they would sleep through the night. That night, he came with a burlap sack and quickly placed all the roosters in his sack and took them to the slaughterhouse. Of course, Donald and I wouldn't think of eating our "pet" chickens. Steve had to take the slaughtered chickens to friends and beg them to take them. Needless to say, this was the last time Steve bought Easter chicks for Donald!

CHAPTER 3: The Call of Community Service

One of the most memorable moments of my life was traveling to Washington, D.C. in January 1961 to attend the inauguration of President Kennedy. Steve and I had received an invitation because we had been active local Linn County volunteers for his 1960 campaign for President. The weather was extremely cold, and our tickets did not allow for much of a view of the ceremony, but Steve and I were very proud that even though we had been born in China and were fairly new American citizens, we still had been invited to the inauguration of the President. That says a lot about the United States.

In his Inaugural Address, President Kennedy said what would turn out to be his most famous words, "Ask not what your country can do for you. Ask what you can do for your country."

Those words reminded me of the advice given by Barnard College President Millicent McIntosh. One of the most important reasons why I wanted to share my memories in this book is that I hope that my grandchildren and anyone reading it will remember the words of Mrs. McIntosh and President Kennedy and that you will find a way to be involved in the decision making process for the benefit of your community. In doing so, you will truly be doing something for your country—and in the long run, for yourself, too. You will find that you will receive much more than you ever give.

I had the privilege of serving in elected office for thirty-nine years. I ran for school boards three times and the state legislature eight times and am proud to have never lost an election. I am proud to have become the first Chinese-American woman in the United States to be elected to a state legislature. I am proud of the bridges I helped to build between my beloved adopted country and my mother country. I am proud to have served my community and my state. Above all, I am proud that during all my time in office I remained true to my principles—the core values that were taught to me by my parents and at school: kindness, harmony and character perfection; love of family, value of lifelong learning, and respect and kindness for fellow men and women.

You don't have to run for office to serve your community. No matter where you live, there will be many volunteer opportunities that will allow you to help make your community a better place in which to live, work, and raise a family. In fact, my community service and political career began by bringing cookies to the classrooms of my son's elementary school!

It all began innocently enough in Albany when Donald and Daniel were in Clover Ridge Elementary School. One day in February, one of their teachers called and asked if I could bring cookies to the classroom for Valentine's Day. I was tempted to say "no," because—as I've already admitted—I'm not a very good cook. I also was very busy in supervising the construction of our new house. But then I remembered what Mrs. McIntosh had said about being involved in your community, and I decided that if the teacher was asking for my help, I needed to say "yes." So I made a batch of cookies. And every time after that, when Donald's or Daniel's teacher would ask me to do something—serve as a room mother or a Cub Scout Den Mother, chaperone a field trip to the zoo, coordinate cooking hot dog lunches, become involved in the parents-teachers club—my answer was always "yes"—no matter how busy I was.

Things got a little more serious when one of the secretaries at the elementary school mentioned to me that there was an opening on the school board, and asked if I was interested in serving. Before I could answer, she suggested that I attend a meeting of the board to see what it was like. I went to a meeting, and I was appalled. The board members were all men, and they spent what seemed like an hour talking about which model of riding lawn mower the school should purchase, and devoted only five minutes to a discussion about not renewing employment of a teacher whon I thought was the best teacher in the school as she was one of the few who actually assigned homework. I was so frustrated with the board's decision that I returned to their next meeting with a petition signed by neighborhood parents asking them to reconsider the non-renewal decision. After they refused to do so, I decided to run for the open seat. A few months later, I won the election.

The promise I made during my campaign was that as a member of the school board, I would work to see that the students received a high quality education. I also made clear that quality education did not have to be expensive, and that every tax dollar needed to be spent wisely. In other words, I wanted to achieve maximum results with the minimum amount of tax dollars. It didn't take me long on the board to realize that I would have a challenging time delivering on that promise. It was obvious to me that many proposed spending increases were not justified. I always cast a "no" vote on budget proposals that exceeded the inflation rate plus enrollment increases, and I voted "no" when proposed expansion of school buildings was not justified by a projected enrollment increase.

When my first five-year term on the elementary school board came to an end in 1974, I asked Donald and Daniel whether I should run again. At that time, Donald was a junior in college and Daniel a sophomore at a college preparatory boarding school in the east coast. They asked me if I was being effective, and I told them I was not. I was on the losing end of many votes, and that since some of my fellow board members were very rude and dismissive to me, I often just quietly voted "no," without explaining the reasons behind my vote or trying to change their minds.

Donald and Daniel both urged me to run again—but only if I promised to be more straightforward and direct in dealing with other board members and in explaining my votes. Their advice was very helpful, and I decided to run for a second term. As I talked to voters during the campaign, I discovered that voters appreciated my work and my fiscal prudence, and I was easily re-elected to the Clover Ridge Elementary School Board for a second term.

Several months later, I was reading the local Albany newspaper and noticed an article about the five candidates who were running for an open position on the Albany High School Board. None of the candidates struck me as highly qualified and none discussed a goal of achieving quality education within the taxpayers' ability to pay, so I decided to throw my hat into the ring. The other candidates included the Chairman of the Oregon State Parole Board, a community college business instructor, a mail carrier, and two housewives.

In my campaign appearances, interviews, and newspaper advertisements I stated that quality education did not have to be expensive, and that our schools should focus on the basics and encourage students to work hard and be motivated to do their best. I won the election by a large margin—gaining 1,085 votes—400 more than my nearest opponent.

Later that year, students came before the high school board to ask for permission to conduct a survey to see if there could be an outdoor area that would be designated for cigarette smoking. This was at a time when smoking was much more accepted than it is today. I said that allowing smoking by students on school grounds was a very bad policy, and made no sense, given that in their health class they were being taught that smoking was a health hazard. I was amazed that I was the only "no" vote against allowing the survey. The local newspaper reported on the vote, and I was pleased that there were many letters to the editor in support of my position.

I was in the newspapers again a few months later when the high school budget came before the board. The request from the superintendent was for a 13.6% budget increase and included $40,000 to purchase land for a proposed new school. This proposed budget increase was nearly twice the increase in the cost of living, and the land acquisition request was made even though student enrollment was decreasing. Therefore, I voted "no."

The superintendent also presented the board with five thick voluminous books of school curriculum, and asked us for our approval. I objected to a vote, saying that if the board was to do our job, then we needed some time—perhaps a month—to review the curriculum before we gave our approval. Much to my amazement, the board approved the curriculum that very evening—without any review at all.

Remembering my conversation with Donald and Daniel about not being afraid to speak out, I made my frustrations very clear. "We're here to provide checks and balances," I said. "If we don't do that, then we might as well go home and watch TV." That quote, along with a photograph of me, was included the next day in the story the local newspaper ran about the meeting.

The more I thought about what the board had done, the more frustrated I was. I wrote a letter to the editor of the Albany newspaper, expressing my concerns with the budget, the land acquisition, and the lack of review of the curriculum, and urged all those who agreed with me to attend the next school board meeting to support my proposal of a curriculum review committee made up of parents, teachers, students and board members. I was delighted the next week when the meeting room was filled with about 100 people, with most speaking in favor of my positions. Unfortunately, the majority of the board would not change their mind.

My frustrations led me to think about quitting the school board, and I sought out a friend and respected county commissioner to ask his advice. He told me that in politics you win some and you lose some and when you lose, you just keep persevering, and eventually you will win. I took his advice to heart and did not resign.

His advice to not give up and to keep persevering would come in very useful during my 26 years in the Oregon State Legislature. And I believe my service in the legislature would not have occurred had I not persevered in the face of setbacks during my time on the school boards.

It was in the spring of 1976—soon after the tussle over the high school budget and curriculum review—when the Linn County Democrat Party Chairman called and asked if I would run for the Oregon House of Representatives. I told him I had no interest in becoming a politician. The Chairman did not take no for an answer, and he invited Steve and me to come to his house for dinner. There, he laid out his case. My service on the school boards and my standing up for students, parents and taxpayers had made me well known, he said. He told us that I was the only Democrat who had a chance of beating Bill Gwinn, the powerful seven-term Republican incumbent. He said that the House of Representatives could use a voice like mine. With Steve's very strong support and encouragement, I reluctantly decided to run.

There were less than eight months between March 17th, the day I officially filed for State Representative, and Election Day on November 2nd. Roger Reid, a good Democrat friend who was an astute Albany attorney, advised me that the best way to campaign was to visit voters at their doors. I listened to his advice, and spent a good share of those months walking door to door in the legislative district—Roger even sent his Republican law clerk to start canvassing door-to-door with me. I shook more hands than I could count, and I discovered that people really liked it when I asked them for their thoughts and concerns, took notes of what they said, and followed up with a prompt response. I was also fortunate that Jeanne Dost, Director of Women's Studies at Oregon State University, volunteered to co-chair my campaign committee and provided a great deal of help, especially in the Benton County portion of my legislative district.

There were also a number of debates with my Republican opponent. In these debates, I advanced the same principles I did during my service on the school boards— "Government and schools needs to live within their income, the same as families and businesses do. They need to set priorities and be accountable for their services and spending." I promised hard work, honesty, and common sense.

While I was campaigning, there were times when I secretly wished that I would lose. There was just so much to learn about so many complex topics. But when I felt like not going door-to-door for the day, I just thought back to the words of Millicent McIntosh, and I thought about how much I owed this country. It was America that helped me during my time of need, and even provided the money that allowed me to attend Barnard during my senior year and to graduate. Remembering what America had done for me at my time of need was the thought that always got me out of the house and back on the campaign trail, brochures and notebook in hand.

I was lucky that for a good portion of the campaign my opponent thought he could win without working very hard. He was complacent and was confident that his name familiarity and the endorsement of local newspapers and various lobbying organizations would translate to victory. Near the end of October, he was surprised when polls came out showing that the race was very close. He immediately sent out three direct mailings to voters in the district, but it was too little, too late. His impersonal mailings couldn't match my personal door-to-door campaigning. I won by 593 votes, with 51.7% of the vote.

CHAPTER 4: **Twenty-six years in the Legislature**

Little did I know that when I raised my hand and took the oath of office as an Oregon State Representative in January 1977, that my service in the legislative arena would span twenty-six years!

Even though the Oregon State Legislature met in regular session from January-July of every odd numbered year—the responsibilities of representing the citizens of my district created a full-time job for 365 days every year. It seemed I was always attending meetings, reading legislation, answering letters, making phone calls, or doing research in support of a constituent request.

Let me give you a quick summary of what my schedule was like when the legislature was in session:

I would usually get up about 5:00a.m. to preview my schedule and to read the legislation that would be up for discussion in one of my committees or on the floor of the chamber. (I guarantee you that I was one of the few members who read every bill before casting a vote on them!)

By 7:30 a.m. or so, I would be on the road, making the 30-minute drive from our home in Albany to the State Capitol in Salem.

Most legislative committees met in the morning, and I usually participated in committee hearings from about 8:30a.m. until 10:30a.m. Following committee meetings, I would hurry back to my office to meet with the many students and constituents from my district who would visit the Capitol. The House or Senate would then typically begin their floor session at 11:00a.m. until noon. During the busy times near the end of session, we would convene earlier and meet all day. I would grab a very quick lunch in the lounge provided for House and Senate members, and then my afternoon would be full of more meetings and committee hearings.

Each legislator is entitled to hire one secretary and one research assistant to help with the work of legislative sessions, and at 5:00p.m. or so, I would meet with my staff to review the day, to assign work, and to look at the schedule for the coming days. Once evening arrived, I would often stay in Salem to attend dinners or receptions sponsored by business and trade organizations, and then would go back to the office to return the many phone calls that came in during the course of a day, and to personally respond to the countless letters I received. I was always the last one to leave the Capitol to go home every night, when I would drive back to Albany, usually arriving home and in bed around midnight, just in time to get a few hours of sleep before repeating the whole schedule the next day! It was a packed 19-hour day, every Monday through Friday!

Weekends were a bit more relaxed, but to make sure that I was providing the best possible representation to my constituents, I also opened small district offices in Albany, Lebanon and Sweet Home, and rotated my attendance among them. I let it be known that anyone who wanted to see me could make an appointment from 9:00a.m. to noon on Saturdays. When I was shopping or out to dinner with Steve, there were countless occasions where I was approached by someone wanting to share their opinion on legislation, or asking for my assistance with a problem they were having with a government agency.

To help me with the work, I hired an aide to send legislation to people in my district who would be impacted by proposed legislation and invited their input. Sending these packets required me to personally pay additional postage beyond the postage allowance provided to legislators, but I believed it was well worth the cost. I also wrote bi-weekly newsletters and end of session reports and provided them to local newspapers so that citizens would be informed about happenings in the legislature.

As you can see, serving as a "part-time" legislator was really a "full-time" job. This is especially true because for the vast majority of my time in the Oregon Legislature I served on the Joint Ways and Means Committee and the "Emergency Board." The Ways and Means Committee was responsible for setting the budgets for the state government and all state agencies. The Emergency Board was a small group of legislators who were empowered with the authority to make needed adjustments to the budget when the legislature was not in session. Serving on these committees meant more hours devoted to reading and studying budgets, and many more hours of meetings. I enjoyed the work, as it allowed me to do what I could to make sure that the tax dollars of my constituents and all Oregonians were wisely spent. It also meant that I received more attention from the state agencies whenever I asked to meet with them regarding constituent concerns, because the agencies knew I could exert power over their budgets. I was especially proud that in the 1997 session, when Republicans controlled the Senate by a 20-10 majority, the Republican President of the Senate named me as the only Democrat Senator on the Ways and Means Committee.

There were numerous times during my legislative years when I would ask myself whether it was all worth it. Was it worth the long days, the late nights, the time away from my family and my home? Every time I asked myself that question, the answer was always "yes." In the pages to come, I will share with you memories and stories of my time in the Oregon State Capitol, and I hope it will explain to you why serving in the legislature was worth all the sacrifices.

I know I don't have to tell you that many young people today are turned off by politics and by politicians. I believe one of the reasons for this is that too many elected officials say one thing during their campaign, and then vote a different way once they are in office. I am proud to tell you that no one could ever make that accusation about me. From my first legislative campaign in 1976 until my last day as a State Senator in 2003, I was very clear in explaining my principles and in remaining true to those principles.

During my twenty-six years in the Oregon State Legislature, I voted on thousands of bills and proposals, and dealt with countless more issues that crossed my desk. While I felt my responsibility was to understand every bill and every issue, there were five priorities which I felt were the most important for the citizens of my district and of Oregon.

Priority #1: Reflecting the needs of the citizens of my district and solving their problems with state government

While I had strong opinions on policy matters, I always believed my primary job as a legislator was to reflect the needs of the people of my district and solve problems they might have with state agencies.

As you know, I am a registered Democrat. But I saw my party registration as far less important than the fact that I was sent to Salem to represent all the people of my district, and not to represent just one party. A challenge I faced from my first day in the legislature to the last was the fact that I was one of the very few Democrat legislators

28

who represented a rural area. The vast majority of the members of the House and Senate Democrat caucus represented urban areas like the cities of Portland, Salem, and Eugene.

One of my very first actions as a new legislator in 1977 was to meet with Representative Phil Lang, the Democrat Speaker of the House, to let him know that among my top priorities was the passage of legislation that would continue to allow farmers in my district to annually burn their fields, a procedure that killed pests, controlled disease, and stimulated growth of the grass seed crop without the use of chemical sprays. Speaker Lang was from Portland, however, and let me know that he supported a ban on field burning, as he believed it was not good for the environment. Lang's decision to not allow a hearing on proposals to continue field burning dismayed other rural legislators, as well, and as the session neared conclusion, seven of us—we called ourselves the "Hornets"— united behind a successful effort to diminish the rule-making power of the Speaker's office and to ensure that legislation important to rural Oregonians would be allowed a hearing. Field burning legislation that was agreeable to my constituents was eventually passed.

As a result of this action and others over my legislative career, I was always regarded as a "swing vote" in the legislature—someone who did not just vote with their political party 100% of the time. This fact did make some of my Democrat colleagues angry with me at times. There were those who thought my job was to vote "the party line," even if that meant voting against the needs and wishes of my district. And when I didn't vote the party line, they occasionally tried to get even with me by denying me my requested committee assignments, or by blocking legislation I proposed.

While the behavior of colleagues did surprise and sadden me on occasions, I steadfastly refused to give in and voted against the official Democrat "party line," when I did not think it was in the best interests of my district. The fact that I never lost an election and was routinely re-elected by overwhelming majorities, proved to me that I was doing exactly the right thing.

My efforts on behalf of the citizens of my district also helped me to quickly develop a reputation that I am proud to say would stay with me throughout my 26 years of legislative service—and that is my reputation as a tireless "bulldog" and "female Davey Crockett" for my constituents. Nothing gave me more pleasure or satisfaction as a legislator than to be able to cut some bureaucratic red tape and make things right for an individual or business in my district.

Of the literally thousands of cases that crossed my legislative desk, there are a few that stand out in my memory. In October 1977, I was approached by Jin Lee, an Albany electrician, who had tried with no avail for thirteen years to bring his wife and two sons from China to America. I enlisted help from our U.S. Congressman's office in pressing his case with China, but that yielded no result. Fortunately, I had already scheduled a visit to China, and while there, I personally met with Mrs. Lee and went to the Ministry of Overseas Chinese Affairs in Hong Kong, and asked them to help. Upon returning to Oregon, I continued to write the Ministry, and was delighted in February 1979 when Mr. Lee was reunited with his family. Seeing the happiness on the faces of the Lee family when they were together again made all the work worthwhile.

Another emotional family reunion for one of my constituents came about after I took their case to the very highest levels of the federal government—the Vice President of the United States! Cyndi Valero of Albany met her husband, Jose, when he was studying fisheries at Oregon State University. They were married, had a daughter, and after Jose received his OSU diploma in 1993, they moved to South Carolina, where Jose would attend the University of Charleston and receive his Master degree. Jose had come to the United States on a scholarship that required he return to Honduras for two years after finishing his education, so Jose, Cyndi, and their young daughter, Amanda, then moved to Honduras. Because of difficult living conditions there, Cyndi and Amanda soon returned to the United States. When Jose's two-year commitment to work in Honduras ended, Cyndi filed papers with the Immigration and Naturalization Service to bring him to the United States. She was told that because of a heavy backlog, processing of the paperwork would take at least six months. That's when Cyndi turned to me for help.

When a story about Cyndi and Jose appeared in the Albany Democrat Herald, a constituent contacted me with a suggestion. He had read that President Bill Clinton and Vice President Al Gore were to be in Portland in a matter of days, and that I should obtain their support in cutting the red tape that was delaying Jose's return. The President and Vice President would be attending a summit on timber issues, and the Vice President would be headlining a fundraiser for the Oregon Democrat Party. I had not planned on attending the fundraiser, but I determined that would provide the best location to make my case. I invited Cyndi to attend with me, and after Vice President Gore gave his speech, we were able to talk briefly with him, and Cyndi presented him with a letter describing the situation. Three weeks later, Cyndi received word that Jose's application has been approved, and Cyndi, Jose, and Amanda soon had an emotional and happy reunion at the Portland International Airport.

Then there was the case of Donny Nealon, who owned a gas station and automobile repair shop in the community of Brownsville. For several years, Donny's business faced a very difficult problem. Whenever there was heavy rain—and it does rain a great deal in Oregon—a huge pool of knee-deep water would build up on an intersection of a state highway and a city street in front of his service station and would not drain away. Donny finally had enough, and decided someone should fix the drainage problem. The city officials in Brownsville said it was Linn County's problem. Linn County officials told him it was the state's problem and to deal with the Oregon Department of Transportation. ODOT directed him back to the City of Brownsville. Donny was incredibly frustrated, and he finally called to ask for my help.

One of the responsibilities of the state legislature is that we set and approve budgets for the various state agencies, so when I called the Oregon Department of Transportation and explained my interest in the issue, things suddenly began to happen. Before Donny knew it, thirteen ODOT employees in nine vehicles showed up at his gas station to assess the drainage problem. I then gathered city, county, and state officials for a meeting to work out a solution to Donny's problem. It was just several months later when improvements were made to the city for Main Street that solved Donny's drainage problem, once and for all. The local Brownsville newspaper printed a story about my successful effort on Donny's behalf and a photograph of the two of us admiring his new drain. The headline of the story was "The Squeaky Wheel Gets the Grease." I am very proud of the fact that I was able to help many citizens like Donny by paying attention to their "squeaks" for help.

ODOT was on top of my call list, as well, when Christian Kim contacted me about the fact that a state road-paving project had turned his Speedy Mart convenience store into an inconvenience store. Prior to the paving project, customers were able to pull up next to the curb in front of the store, and they could quickly dash in to make a purchase. After the paving project, however, much of the close-by parking was eliminated. He called ODOT to ask them for help, but said that "They were pretty government about it." He then gave up, and saw his business drop off for a number of years. An employee of Mr. Kim's then suggested that he call me. He explained his dilemma, and I called ODOT. Much to my and Mr. Kim's delight, they came up with a plan that returned three parking spaces near the front of the store.

I also remember an occasion where a letter from a constituent led to a much- needed change in state policy. In July 1990, the Oregon Department of Human Resources announced they were scrapping a new $12.5 million computer system that its employees could not operate. A few days later, I received a letter from Bob Beil of Albany, expressing his frustration with this waste of tax dollars. Based on this letter, I invited Human Resource officials to Albany to explain this snafu to Bob and other interested citizens. While they couldn't turn the clock back, they did announce that the new computer system would be modeled after one that other states had installed and that had proven successful.

I never imagined serving in the legislature would make me an expert on propane gas, but in November, 1991, the manager and staff of an Albany propane gas company came to see me regarding legislation passed into law in the 1991 session that increased fees on businesses handling and storing hazardous substances. Under the legislation, the State Fire Marshall was authorized to identify all businesses subject to the fee. The new fee would then be set based on the number of businesses identified, with the intent of charging higher fees to the larger businesses or higher users, thereby allowing businesses that only kept a small amount of hazardous materials to be exempted or to pay a proportionately lower fee. My constituents were frustrated that the Fire Marshall had vastly under identified the number of businesses handling and storing hazardous substances and was not listening to their concerns.

The final amount of the fee was to be approved at the December 3, 1991 Emergency Board meeting. I quickly met with the two co-chairs of the legislative emergency board, Senate President Kitzhaber and House Speaker Campbell. I had to chase the Speaker to the Capitol parking garage—to explain the situation. At the E-Board meeting, I successfully argued for a delay in the fee assessment until a more thorough count was made. As it turned out, my constituents were correct, and the number of businesses had been undercounted. I was informed in February, 1992 that prior to my involvement, those businesses with storage of less than 7000 gallons of propane gas would have faced an average annual bill of $600, and following the new count, the annual registration fee was reduced to $25. The savings to Oregon businesses using propane to heat their offices and facilities or for industrial applications like powering forklifts could well be in the range of several hundred thousand dollars annually. The propane gas association thanked me in a letter, writing that I was proof that "democracy works if government representatives take people's wishes seriously."

Another cost saving idea that I took seriously was that of Albany Dr. Jack Lees, who met with me before the 1979 legislative session to make the common sense suggestion that non-smokers should pay lower health insurance rates than smokers. I sponsored legislation that led to the creation of the nation's first health insurance policy with a 10% non-smoker discount, thereby providing an economic incentive for policyholders to adopt a healthier lifestyle.

A memorable "squeaky wheel" story that is one of my favorites occurred in September 1987 when Don Rhodewalt, a resident of the small community of Scio, called and asked me to speak at a rally to save the Weddle Bridge, a 50-year old covered bridge that was slated for demolition. In preparation for the speech, I did some research, and learned that Oregon was home to 49 covered bridges, which ranked us first in the western United States and fifth in the nation in the number of standing covered bridges. I was also alarmed to discover, however that in 1938 there were 300 covered bridges in 1959 there were 105, and in 1987 there were only 49. We had lost approximately 250 bridges in 50 years!

There was no doubt that covered bridges were fast becoming an "endangered species." I concluded that the Weddle Bridge and Oregon's other covered bridges were historic sites, and that they should be maintained so future generations could enjoy them.

While it was too late to save the Weddle Bridge from being dismantled—although it was later reassembled and restored in the Linn County community of Sweet Home, I was able to obtain state funding from the Joint Legislative Emergency Board, on which

I served, for a study of all of Oregon's covered bridges. The study analyzed the condition of Oregon's covered bridges, determined their importance to transportation and tourism, and also estimated the cost of maintaining the bridges and recommended sources of funds to pay for repairs. In subsequent legislative sessions, I was able to utilize this study to obtain state and lottery funding for repair, restoration and maintenance of covered bridges across Oregon. Owners of the covered bridges—mostly county governments—were required to provide matching funds or in-kind contributions for the projects.

I am very proud of the fact that there is a plaque on the Weddle Bridge presented by the Oregon Society of Covered Bridges, the Cascade Resource Group in Sweet Home and the Linn County Covered Bridge Association that pays tribute to my efforts. The placement of the plaque on the Weddle Bridge is most appropriate, as that is where it all started.

The plaque reads as follows:

"State Senator Mae Yih became involved with the state's 49 covered bridges in 1987. Through her legislative efforts, she has been responsible for:

Obtaining $450,000 in funding for the bridges during the 1989 to 1991 biennium.

Obtaining $470,000 in funds for the bridges during the 1991-93 biennium.

Obtaining $370,000 in funds for the bridges during the 1993-95 biennium.

Creation and passage of Senate Bill 273, which provided protection for the bridges.

Presented by the Oregon Society of Covered Bridges, the Cascades Forest Resource Group, Linn County Covered Bridge Association and private citizens."

Also, if you go to the website of the Covered Bridge Society of Oregon, you will find this entry about the Weddle Bridge:

"The Weddle Covered Bridge is a typical example of Linn County's open-sided covered bridges. Many Linn County residents believed that this bridge was lost forever when it was yanked apart by workers in October 1987. The bridge had spanned Thomas Creek for 50 years.

It was bypassed in 1980 by a concrete bridge downstream, and neglected. The deteriorated bridge eventually became a safety issue, and the span was scheduled to be demolished.

This action sparked protests by local covered bridge enthusiasts. As the story goes, one person chained himself to a bulldozer to prevent the bridge's demise.

The covered bridge enthusiasts engaged Senator Mae Yih, a local legislator who became a leader in saving Oregon's covered bridges. Through her efforts, the Oregon Legislature created the Oregon Covered Bridge Program which helped fund covered bridge maintenance and rehabilitation projects throughout the state."

My efforts to save Oregon's covered bridges led to my selection in March 1992 as Chair of the Covered Bridges Advisory Committee. The committee was established by the 1991 Legislature to set up an annual inspection program and make recommenda-tions for rehabilitating and maintaining the covered bridges in Oregon. The legislature also allocated gas tax money and lottery funds to help pay for the necessary expenses.

Another bridge received my attention later in November 1991 when a bridge cross-ing the Santiam River that led to the Cascadia State Park in my district was deemed unsafe and closed by Oregon State Parks Department. Local citizens were worried that the route to an alternate bridge went through the heart of the community, endangering children who often played close to the road. Further, the alternate bridge crossing—a narrow substandard gravel road—was difficult to reach, and would likely lead to de-creased usage of the park, harming local businesses that depended upon visits from some of the over 100,000 people who visited the park each year. Cascadia Park was well known for its stand of old growth timber, its waterfalls, Indian cave, historic trails and soda springs, which had been sought for their medicinal purposes for many years. Additionally, the bridge to be closed was of a "Howe Truss" design, one of only two bridges of this design remaining in the United States.

I visited the closed bridge and the residents of the small community of 200 people and concurred with their deep concern regarding safety and their loss of direct access to the main Highway 20. I immediately requested that officials from the state parks and transportation departments and the county road department come to my Salem office to meet with local citizens.

Our ultimate goal was to repair the bridge if possible, or to build a permanent safe replacement. Eight meetings later, we achieved the first steps to that goal, when in Feb-ruary 1992 the state parks division announced that they would install a temporary bridge in time for the summer tourist season, and that a plan to build a permanent bridge with federal historic bridges restoration funds had been approved. Cascadia Bridge would be replaced by a nearly exact replica of the original timber bridge and constructed in line with more stringent seismic design codes and could withstand higher stress levels from modern traffic loads. It was projected to have at least a 50-year life.

In July 1992, I was delighted to attend a ceremony at the park, marking the park's 50th anniversary, and officially opening a new temporary bridge. I would return nearly two years later to join in cutting the ribbon at a ceremony officially dedicating the new permanent bridge. I told those gathered that "the bridge was a shining example of how we can bring concerned citizens and different levels of government together to work out a solution." I was very flattered by the kind words spoken by a local resident, who said, "This has been the greatest thing to happen to Cascade in 30 years. We lost our school, we lost our gas station, and without the bridge and the park, we'd lose our only grocery store." Jean Burger, the leader of the Cascadia Bridge Restoration Group, said I had restored residents' faith in a community that had long felt forgotten. She described me as "a little package of dynamite!"

Protecting Oregon's historic bridges would remain on my agenda throughout my service in the Oregon State Legislature, and I was successful as a senior member of the Ways and Means Committee in fighting for state highway and lottery funds to pay for continued restoration and maintenance of these treasures.

Another bridge in my district moved to the top of my agenda on January 29, 2001 when parts of a tall crane being towed across the Harrisburg Bridge struck the bridge's supports, causing more than $300,000 in damage and closing the bridge for two weeks. The closure proved to be a significant burden to Harrisburg businesses and residents, as what was once a twelve-minute trip from Harrisburg to Junction City across the bridge became a 60-minute trip with the new route required by the closure. The closure could have been avoided if the bridge had a warning system that would alert drivers if their loads were too high for the bridge. I was able to convince the Oregon Department of Transportation to install the advance warning system on the Harrisburg Bridge at the City of Halsey so drivers can take a different route if their loads were too high for the bridge. Loyd Henion, a constituent of mine who worked as an economist for the Oregon Department of Transportation, suggested the electronic warning system. I often sought his advice on transportation issues during my years in the legislature, and he always offered insightful and unbiased expert analysis and recommendations.

I am also proud that I was able to play a small role in helping to save a historic home in Brownsville. The Moyer House was built in 1881 by an early Brownsville businessman and mill owner, and was one of Oregon's finest surviving examples of Italianate Victorian architecture. A group of local citizens invited me to an informal meeting at the house, where they listed the repairs and improvements that needed to be made as part of a $135,000 restoration project. The home was a historical treasure that needed to be preserved for future generations, and I was happy to be able to obtain state historic preservation funds to assist in the restoration.

While my legislative district had some beautiful and historic bridges and buildings, it also had miles and miles of highways that were critical to both the local and state economy. In 1988, I devoted a great deal of time to ensuring that the highways in my district were included in a state transportation six-year plan that ensured the highways would be eligible to receive gas tax money for much needed improvements. Initially, these highways—which connected the mid-Willamette Valley with Oregon's coast and with central Oregon, were excluded from the list. When I saw that exclusion, I decided it was time for me to be a "squeaky wheel," and to recruit other "squeaky wheels."

I contacted elected officials and businesses from across Linn County to inform them of the exclusion and to invite them to a hearing on the transportation plan that the Oregon Transportation Commission would soon be holding. When the day of the hearing arrived, over 150 officials, business executives, workers, farmers, and concerned citizens joined me in packing the room, signing a petition to the commission and the governor, and in making very clear how important it was for the economic health and the safety of Linn County that our highways be included in the statewide improvement plan. Two weeks later, the Chairman of the Oregon Transportation Commission and Governor Goldschmidt told me that the strong community support and convincing testimonies had made the difference and resulted in Linn County being included in the final plan!

Highway safety was also on my agenda in 1993, when an October 4th auto accident at the intersection of Oakville Road and Highway 34 in Linn County claimed the life of a 16-year old youth. This was the ninth fatal accident in six years at the intersection. Residents and business owners enlisted my immediate concern and urge the State Highway Division to install a traffic light at the dangerous intersection of Highway 34 and Oakville Road. I brought the mother of the teenager killed in the accident with me to meet with officials at the accident site and to make our case. The officials explained that there was a policy against putting traffic lights up in rural areas, but they promised an immediate study of traffic counts. I continued to press the case for a traffic light. I called the Director of the Oregon Department of Transportation, testified before the Transportation Commission, and I also met with the local patrol officers of the Oregon State Police. After that meeting the State Police announced plans to designate a portion of Highway 34 as a state "traffic safety corridor," a designation that meant lower speed limits, more traffic signs, and increased police patrols.

In December 1993, state transportation officials told me they had a new plan to improve safety at the intersection, and I invited the public to join me in a meeting where they would explain their plan. Their plan included a new turn around/refuge lane at the dangerous intersection, limiting drivers to cross the highway only two lanes at a time rather than four lanes at a time, and the hiring of additional state police officers to patrol Highway 34. While the concerned citizens and I continued to believe that a traffic light would be more effective (and cost $500,000 less than a rebuilt intersection), we gave their plan our support, and the intersection was rebuilt the following summer.

There was another traffic safety issue that led me to receive some ribbing from legislative lobbyists. After being contacted by senior constituents in Lebanon and Sweet Home, I introduced legislation during the 1999 session that would have required the Oregon Department of Transportation to install traffic signals that would assist blind pedestrians. These signals, which were in use in other states, were activated by a button that emitted "bird chirps" to indicate when it was safe to cross. My bill required these signals to be installed upon request by people who needed them and where neighborhood approval was granted. I thought these audible signals would be of great help to the visually impaired. Lobbyists, however, chuckled at the "cuckoo" (for north-south) and "peep" (for east-west) sounds emitted by the signals and declared it the "turkey bill of the year."

Another transportation project I enjoyed working on was one that paid tribute to the first transcontinental automobile race, which was the 1905 race from New York City to Portland. A nineteen mile section of the road used in that race was Old Santiam Road in Eastern Linn County, and was being restored by the United States Forest Service to turn of the century condition. The restored road was restricted for use to cyclists, horseback riders, and antique cars. The 1905 race was between two Oldsmobiles and lasted 44 days. The race wound through eleven states and entered Oregon at Ontario. They then traveled to Sisters, and headed west on the historic Santiam Wagon Road. Drivers Dwight Huss and Percy Megargel guided their cars through torrential rains and undeveloped, muddy, rocky roads. They forged rivers, fell through wooden bridges, maneuvered through axle deep mud and suffered frequent breakdowns. Tales were even told that the automobiles were rescued by covered wagons still making their way across the Oregon Trail! Actually, the Olds Runabout was the first automobile to travel coast to coast, the first to cross the Cascades, and the first to traverse the Oregon Trail.

About 200 people gathered on Old Santiam road on July 7, 1995 for a dedication at Lost Prairie Campground of a historical marker commemorating the 90th anniversary of the race and the restoration of the 130-year-old Santiam Wagon Road. The guests included John Huss, the son of Dwight Huss, who was the winning driver of the race! In the 1995 legislative session, I was able to obtain lottery funding to help pay for the video documentary of the historic race. I believed this investment would be paid back many times as the documentary would lead to increased tourism from the public, especially educators, historians, antique car owners, race enthusiasts, horseback riders, and cyclists. The film producer completed his project in 1998 and I was invited to join him at a ceremony in Sweet Home that year where he officially presented Forest Service officials, community leaders, and various organizations with copies of the two hour documentary titled "From Hellgate to Portland"

While I took great pride in advancing projects that strengthened my district's material resources like bridges, buildings and highways, more satisfying were those projects that helped our human resources—especially our young people.

In the late 1980's, I heard many times from experts in my district that there was a near epidemic of youth drug and alcohol addiction issues in Oregon and in my legislative district. The few youth addiction treatment centers in Oregon all had long waiting lists, and some teens were committing suicide while they waited for an opening in a center. I was able to pass legislation for the establishment of new centers, but was unable to get funding for them. However, at the recommendation of my good friend, Senator Mike Thorne, who represented Eastern Oregon, and was Co-Chairman of the Ways and Means Committee, I inserted a budget note in the Department of Human Services budget creating an interim task force to study the need for and the locations of the new adolescent drug treatment centers. I was invited to serve as one of the two legislative members of the task force, and also successfully recommended the appointment of Albany attorney Paul Kuebrick. We were told at the hearing that Oregon adolescents use drugs more frequently and at a younger age than in other states. More than 1,000 Oregon adolescents were on a waiting list for treatment, but only 31 spaces for those programs existed. The task force listened to testimony from police officers, doctors, mental health professionals, school officials, students and parents of children who were involved with drugs and alcohol. Albany Police Chief Pat Marina discussed the lack of facilities to handle teenagers involved in drugs and crime to support their habits. He believed that treatment centers would be far more successful than law enforcement in dealing with these kids. During the interim, I was able to obtain federal and state funding to open the recommended centers and to keep them operating.

One of the centers that opened was the Youth Entering Sobriety (YES) House in Albany, which served the youth from Benton, Linn, Marion, Yamhill, Polk, Lane and Lincoln Counties. Prior to the opening of this residential center, local youth with alcohol and drug problems had to travel 90 minutes to Portland for treatment. I visited the YES House on several occasions, and was always tremendously impressed by the positive difference it made in turning around lives and giving young people hope for a better future. I especially remember a visit I made in 1996 to participate in a celebration that marked the official designation of the YES House as a school drug-free zone. An 18-year-old named Michelle shared the story of how she had battled marijuana and methamphetamine addiction for thirteen months. During that time, she ran away from home, dropped out of school, and was arrested. Finally, she arrived at YES House, which turned her life around. She returned home, received her high school diploma, and planned on attending college and becoming a drug and alcohol counselor. She said that residential treatment centers were effective because she didn't return to her old friends and become addicted again.

Along with working to reduce youth drug and alcohol abuse, I also devoted a great deal of time to advocating policies that would reduce the incidents of teen pregnancy. I believed that the tremendous personal, social, and public costs arising from teen pregnancy required concerted involvement. These costs included the fact that teen mothers were less likely to finish school, were more likely to be on welfare, that studies revealed that 70% of men and women in prison were born to teen parents, and that teen sexual activity accounted for rising cases of sexually transmitted diseases. Each pregnant teen costs Oregon taxpayers an average of $30,000 in lifetime medical and welfare costs. In 1989, the state's outlay attributable to teen childbearing was $174 million.

In 1994, I attended a conference on teen pregnancy prevention sponsored by Governor Roberts, in which they discussed the effectiveness of the Grady Memorial Curriculum, an abstinence based teen pregnancy prevention curriculum issued by Emory University and Grady Memorial Hospital Teen Clinic in Georgia, that had proven successful. In the 1995 legislative session, I introduced a bill urging schools to adopt the Curriculum. The STARS (Students Today Aren't Ready for Sex) curriculum trained high school seniors to discuss with seventh graders why they needed to postpone sexual involvement and also taught "refusal skills." According to senior leaders, middle schoolers were learning about life from people they could relate to. They weren't the only ones learning, as seniors would never forget their mentoring experience. A study by Emory University concluded that students who had not participated in the program were as much as five times more likely to have begun having sex than those who had participated in the program.

After my legislation encouraging schools to adopt the Grady Memorial Curriculum was passed in 1995, $250,000 was allocated to the Oregon Health Division to provide grants to schools to implement programs. In the 1997 session, an additional $350,000 was allocated. Matching federal funds for abstinence education would ensure another $800,000 for the program, resulting in a 700% budget increase to combat teen pregnancy. I met with school administrators in Linn County in 1994, 1995, and 1996 and urged many school districts, including Albany, Lebanon, Sweet Home, Central Linn, Harrisburg and Scio to successfully apply for funding which allowed them to implement the program.

My efforts in teen pregnancy prevention received a boost in 1996, when Sharon Kitzhaber, the Governor's wife, became an advocate for the "STARS" program. Mrs. Kitzhaber joined me in June 1996 in attending a STARS program completion ceremony at South Albany High School, and presenting 16 teen leaders with a certificate. Mrs. Kitzhaber set a goal of ensuring that every Oregon sixth and seventh grader had the opportunity to participate in the STARS program by the year 2000. She also pledged to help raise additional funds from businesses to help finance the program.

I went to bat for STARS again in 2004, after I retired from the legislature, when it was reported that the Albany School District was dropping STARS because, among other reasons, they had doubts about the effectiveness of the program. I was joined by several high school leaders who taught the program in going before the Albany School Board to ask that the program be reinstated.

I presented data regarding the effectiveness of the Grady Memorial curriculum. The data revealed that students who participated in the curriculum were five times less likely to become involved in sex. In Linn County, pregnancies in girls ages 10 to 19 dropped from 17.8 per thousand in 1995 to 12.3 per thousand in 2003. The effectiveness of the program led the Portland, Oregon public schools to increase the number of schools adopting the program from six the first year, to nineteen the second year, to thirty-three the third year.

Several weeks after the hearing, and after many supportive letters to the editor were printed in the newspaper, the Albany School District did restore the program for three years for sixth graders in one middle school. The school was expected to conduct an analysis of whether there were any differences in risky behavior between those students entering high school who received the STARS program and those who didn't.

Another effort of mine for several sessions was strengthening the state's ability to collect child support payments from non-custodial parents. This gained my interest when I met with a constituent who needed assistance in collecting child support. According to the state's child support administrator, 80% of child support payments were delinquent—accounting for some half billion dollars. In the 1993 and 1995 sessions, I introduced legislation to require most employers in industries and businesses to report hiring or rehiring of employees to the Support Enforcement Division of the Oregon Department of Justice within 14 days. The recommendation behind this bill was that child support enforcement agencies had long used quarterly employment tax records in locating parents who owed child support. The problem was that the employment of an individual hired in July, for instance, wouldn't come to the attention of the state until three or four months later, when the report was received. The state—and the custodial parent who needed those payments—were thereby losing out on three or four months of wages that they could attach. And if the job was temporary or seasonal and the employee had already moved on by the time the report was received, then they wouldn't be able to collect support until they found the parent's next employment. Eleven states already had similar systems, and federal legislation mandating the system for all employers was under consideration in the United States Congress.

The business lobby opposed my legislation, stating that the requirement was too burdensome. I pointed out that I had always been a very strong supporter of business and a dire opponent of excessive regulations. In this case, I believed that the burden was minimal, and that the money the state would collect through the new reporting system would greatly assist the custodial parent and children, and would save the state in support costs for families receiving state assistance. My proposal was amended to limit the legislation to certain industries that historically had high employment turnover, the business lobby supported the bill, and it was passed into law for a two-year trial period. During the 1995 legislature, we were presented with evidence that my legislation had worked exactly as intended, as an additional $3 million in delinquent child support payments had been collected, and projections were that number would soon double. Based on this evidence, I introduced legislation to repeal the "sunset provision" that had limited the program to a two-year period, and that expanded the industries included in the program while also simplifying report forms, thereby enabling the Support Enforcement Division to collect $10.8 million more in child support in next biennium. It was unanimously approved.

The successful implementation of my legislation soon led the business lobby to reconsider their opposition. The powerful Associated Oregon Industries even used their 1996 newsletter to encourage all their members to assist in the collection of child support.

During the 1997 session, I moved from writing legislation dealing with child support to writing legislation dealing with spousal support. A woman from Albany came to my office at the beginning of the session and told me that the Public Employee Retiree Benefits (PERS) payment that was being sent to her husband were completely cut off after he passed away. Since she was elderly and had no means of making a living, the PERS benefit payment was desperately needed. PERS employees revealed to her that her husband had excluded her from any benefits upon his death. While it was his legal right to do this, and I couldn't do anything to help my constituent, I was able to bring about the passage of legislation that protected future individuals, by requiring PERS members to obtain their spouses consent in their retirement plans, before they were cut off from spouse's death benefits. PERS members received larger monthly payments if there were no provisions for spouses upon death. My bill only applied to members of PERS because spouses of private retirement plan members were already protected by federal law.

Certainly one of the most unique constituent requests I received was from the individual who wrote me a letter, explaining that she wanted to apply for a pilot's license, and one of the documents required for the license was a birth certificate. She said she wanted to be able to petition the court to make a correction on her birth certificate before she sent in her pilot's license application. Since courts could already legally order name changes on birth certificates, I saw no problem with the request and asked the Office of Legislative Counsel to draft the legislation.

When a committee hearing was scheduled, I contacted my constituent to ask her to testify on the legislation. The first time I saw her was in my office on the morning of the hearing, and I was quite shocked to see a woman over six feet tall towering over me with a tall hairdo and high heels. As we made our way from my office to the committee hearing, we were followed by a crew of television reporters and cameramen who had heard about the unusual legislation. When we arrived at the hearing and sat down at the witness table, the committee chair said that there would be no need for us to testify, and that the committee would support passage of the legislation. I finally realized that my constituent had gone through a sex change operation, and she wanted her birth certificate that stated she was a male, changed to state that she was a female.

The bill passed the full House and was scheduled for a Senate committee hearing. The Senate committee chair also told us that there was no need to testify, and the committee promptly passed the bill. When the bill reached the Senate floor, Senator Ken Jernstedt, who was leading debate on the bill, said it was a good bill that should pass, and suggested that if anyone had questions about the bill, they should be referred to Representative Yih. The bill was easily approved.

Eventually, the bill was signed into law, and the leading newspaper of the state, The Oregonian, published a full-page article about the legislation, praising me for sponsoring historic legislation. In the article, my constituent, who asked that her name remain anonymous, said she considered me as a legislator who represented her constituents in the highest possible manner. She knew that as a conservative Democrat I was risking my reputation to stand up to sponsor the bill for her. But knowing that this step helped to make her a whole person mentally as well as physically after all the difficult procedures she had gone through gave me tremendous satisfaction. This confirmed my belief that when you help someone in need, you really gain more in return than you ever give.

It was a newspaper editor who provided the idea that led to a change in state law in the 2001 session. Hasso Hering, the long-time editor of the Albany Democrat Herald, commented in an editorial that Oregon's ballot measure numbering system was confusing. As I thought about Hasso's comment, I knew that he was right. Every election year, ballot measures would be numbered according to when they received the necessary signatures to be placed on the ballot. And each election year, the numbering began with Ballot Measure #1. So each election year, there was likely to be a Ballot Measure #1, a Ballot Measure #2, a Ballot Measure #3, and so on.

The problem was that some of the Ballot Measures—especially the ones involving subjects like taxation, gun control, and gay rights—were so controversial that they continued to be discussed and written about even after the election year was over. For instance, in 1990, voters passed Ballot Measure 5, which placed a limit on taxes. For many years thereafter, the press would refer to "Measure 5 tax limitations." In 2000, voters expressed confusion with another Measure 5, which required background checks on unlicensed dealers at gun shows. Two recent controversial and much debated Measure 9's dealt separately with campaign finance restrictions and equal rights for the gay and lesbian community. To end any confusion, I authored legislation that required ballot measures to be numbered consecutively without an upper limit, so that each number would only be assigned to one ballot measure. The legislation was passed with support from the Oregon Secretary of State, who was in charge of the election process. When the Governor signed it into law, I made sure that Hasso was there to witness the fact that one person's suggestion can actually lead to a change in law.

Another example of one citizen making a difference in changing law occurred in the 1991 session when a constituent contacted me to say that her insurance company had cancelled her homeowner's insurance because she operated a child care service out of her home. I learned that other child care providers were also seeing similar cancellations, as insurance companies were concerned with the number of child abuse lawsuits filed against child care providers. I introduced and successfully led the effort to pass legislation that provided a safeguard for insurance companies, enabling them to offer homeowners insurance to child care providers without accepting liability for lawsuits resulting from daycare operations. This makes it possible for child care providers to have accessible and affordable homeowner insurance policies.

I also recall being contacted by a senior citizen in 1997 who had a very unique dilemma. The Oregon Department of Transportation had condemned the man's home as part of a highway widening project. The man then moved to another home, and wanted to continue taking advantage of a program that allowed the state to pay the residential property taxes of the homes of senior citizens. The state would then retain a lien on the property in the amount of taxes and accrued interest, and the lien would be paid off upon the sale of the house. State law, however, did not allow senior citizens to transfer this tax deferral from one house to another. Because the state forced my constituent to leave his house for another, he thought he should be granted a waiver from this policy, so that he could continue to use the tax deferral program on his new house. The state said no. I believed my constituent was right, and I drafted an amendment to another proposed bill, allowing for the deferral to be transferred when senior's homes were condemned by the Department of Transportation. The amendment was adopted, the bill was eventually passed into law, and my constituent later wrote a letter to the Albany Democrat Herald stating that he was grateful that I did all the work "for a total stranger."

I am also very proud of an amendment passed by the 1993 legislature that I authored to assist just two Oregonians. William and Marci Rothleutner of Tangent, Oregon, had been required by the Department of Environmental Quality to hook up their home to the Tangent city sewer system in 1987. The couple requested and received a tax credit of $100 a year for five years, and had received the credit for two years, when the Oregon Department of Revenue ruled that the credits were granted in error. The Rothleutners then repaid the $200 credit plus $40 in interest. I was appalled that the state bureaucracy would force the Rothleutners to repay this money, since the state had granted them the credit in the first place. I requested an opinion from Oregon Attorney General Dave Frohnmayer. He agreed with me that the Rothleutners were entitled to the credit, but that the time for appealing their repayment of the credit had expired. Therefore, the only way to reimburse them $240 was to pass legislation permitting their late appeal. We needed to right the wrong of two state agencies, no matter how long ago it happened. And that is just what the legislature did!

My reputation as a watchdog of the budget often led citizens to call me when they saw examples of wasteful government spending. In 1997, a Corvallis architect who was concerned with the state government's practice of building new state agency offices suggested that tax money could be saved if state government inventoried and made use of vacant state buildings rather than building new ones. Given that the state had 6,500 buildings that would cost $3.4 billion to replace and it had no maintenance plan, I thought it was a great idea. I authored legislation requiring state agencies to inventory and consider vacant buildings and other factors in planning for efficient use of space, and was delighted when the bill was enacted and signed into law. Senate Ways and Means Committee Co-Chair Senator Gene Timms told me that he thought it was the best bill of the session.

There were several times when helping my constituents took some quick legislative moves. During the 1993 session, I was contacted by Bill Kiewell, the general manager of the Albany-based National Frozen Foods Corporation. He was concerned that a state law scheduled to go into effect on January 1, 1995 would lead to a possible loss of 500 food processing jobs in Linn County, and a loss of 2,000 jobs statewide. The state law would require that rigid plastic containers sold in Oregon be made of at least 25% recycled or reusable material. The problem was that the federal law required no recycled material in the rigid plastic container, and when the Oregon law went into effect, it would have forced food processors to package products sold in Oregon differently from products sold everywhere else. Mr. Kiewell was joined by many others in industries ranging from food processing to cosmetics to medical equipment to retail groceries in extending the implementation of the law by one year, thereby allowing the 1995 legislature to review the issue again. Supporters of the law insisted for months that they would not change the compliance date.

After hearing Mr. Kiewell's concerns, I sent him to Senator Gordon Smith's office. Senator Smith happened to own a food processing plant in Eastern Oregon and I knew he would understand the situation. Senator Smith also served on the Senate Agriculture and Natural Resources Committee, and I knew he and his caucus would join me in conveying to the Department of Environmental Quality that if the date was not changed, then the DEQ—which was responsible for overseeing the recycling law—would not have its budget approved. Legislation was soon passed to make the one-year change in the compliance date. The DEQ was notorious for overregulation and bureaucracy, and my belief was that it was essential that state agencies work with business and industries for public safety, as well as economic development. Being able to tell them that they had to behave or they wouldn't receive their budget was a highlight of the session for me.

As the 1993 session neared conclusion, Mary and Wally Eicher of Corvallis called me at home during a weekend to explain that a loophole in Oregon law was about to cost them a lot of money. The Eichlers were grass seed straw harvesters, and the legal definition of farming did not include harvesting straw from another person's land. Therefore, straw barns were not considered farm use, and instead of qualifying for farm use tax rates, they would be taxed at the much higher commercial rate and would also be subject to a higher property tax assessment. This news came as the "last straw" to the Eichlers, who were also facing twelve citations from the Public Utility Commission for transporting straw on trucks designated for farm use.

After hearing their surprise news from the assessor's office, I immediately invited the executive directors of the Oregon Departments of Revenue and Agriculture to my office to meet with the Eichlers and to find a solution. With the session almost over, the rules did not permit the introduction of new legislation, but they did permit amending bills that were already in the system. The department heads recommended that HB 2934, which would allow horse training or stabling to be classified as exclusive farm use, and which had been languishing in committee, as the perfect vehicle for my amendment. The committee liked the idea of encouraging straw to be stored and used as export for feed or other applications to reduce field burning. With the addition of my amendment, the bill was passed in the session's final hours. The Horse Council of Oregon, who requested HB 2934, said that "the straw saved the horses." Mary and Wally Eichler declared the "horses saved the straw." I worked with the Eichlers again in 1995 when state bureaucrats decreed that straw hauled from the field to a storage barn and from the storage barn to a bail compressor qualified as "agriculture" and could be done with vehicles with farm license plates, but when the straw left the compressor and headed to market, it had to be transported in a vehicle with commercial plates. This decree meant additional expenses for straw farmers, and I resolved to look for a way to fix it. I was pleased that I was able to convince my legislative colleagues to allow farm plate use for transportation of the straw to Oregon's ports so it could be exported.

In the 1995 session, I turned from horses to deer, elk, and antelope, when a constituent by the name of James Bond made me aware of a problem. Bond made Native American arts and crafts, and while Oregon law allowed for the sale, possession, and use of deer antlers and hides, it did not specifically allow for the use of hooves, claws and sinews, which had been used for centuries in Native American crafts. I introduced legislation in the 1995 session that would allow for the use of this material that would otherwise be wasted, and was passed into law late in the session. Mr. Bond was so pleased with my efforts that for many years at Christmas time he would bring me a big jar of honey and venison sausage.

An example of government "Catch 22" regulation was brought to my attention during the 1997 session by managers of the Smurfit Newsprint Corporation in Sweet Home. They explained to me that Oregon law prevented experienced maintenance workers from performing some routine tasks, like resetting a breaker switch, replacing a broken motor, or changing a fuse. Instead, they had to hire electrical contractors, as the law required that only workers who were qualified as "limited maintenance electricians" (LME) could perform such tasks. The state required two years of experience before a written examination could be taken to become a LME, but the state did not recognize any experience unless it was gained through an apprenticeship program—and there were no such apprenticeship programs in Oregon! In short, someone had to work outside of Oregon in a state with an apprenticeship program, before they could have two years of experience recognized, and take the examination to become an LME in Oregon. Bureaucracy at its worst! Legislation I sponsored to address this problem and to allow individuals with two or more years of supervised electrical maintenance experience to take the written examination was passed overwhelmingly during the 1997 session.

One of the most satisfying constituent problems I helped to solve involved the small community of Millersburg. Before sharing that story, however, I need to tell you that your grandfather was the "father of Millersburg." Back in 1973, Stephen was President of Wah Chang, and two community leaders who also served on the board of Albany General Hospital asked him for a $100,000 corporate donation for the hospital. In return, the men said that the City of Albany would delay what many thought was the inevitable annexation of land that included the Wah Chang industrial site in unincorporated Linn County. Stephen made the donation, as any annexation would mean a dramatic increase in taxes and regulations for Wah Chang. However, not long after the donation was made, city officials made clear that they would soon move to annexation.

The only way to prevent annexation by the City of Albany was to create an independent city. Stephen hired attorneys to draw up papers that incorporated the industrial area into a new city of Millersburg (named after Isaac Miler, an early Oregon pioneer). The incorporation proposal was eventually placed on the ballot for a vote of the area residents in June 1974, and it was victorious by a two vote margin—76 to 74! The victory might have been due to the fact that Stephen was thoughtful enough to have provided car pool transportation for people who needed rides to the polling place

Twenty years later, *The Oregonian* published a story detailing the history of Millersburg and the remarkable benefits it offered to citizens and businesses. In 1994, Millersburg had a population of 720 and three major businesses had operations in Millersburg—Wah Chang, Willamette Industries and Georgia Pacific. These three businesses saved roughly $1.1 million annually by not being part of Albany, which charged more for city services and taxes. Millersburg charged franchise fees to the utilities who serviced the three major businesses. These fees yielded more than enough money to fund city operations, and meant that the citizens of the city did not have to pay any property taxes. Further, the city paid 80% of its residents' costs to participate in sports or recreation programs in Albany, with a limit of $200 per family, it paid $35 of the $40 cost of a library card in the Albany public library, and, most impressively, it paid up to $3,000 a year toward college tuition for Millersburg students who graduated from high school in Albany. (There were no schools in Millersburg.) It's no wonder that Millersburg is called "the richest little town in Oregon."

Millersburg did have one problem that had persisted for thirty-five years—in periods of unusually frequent and heavy rain, it became one of the wettest little towns in Oregon, with flooding occurring on the I-5 freeway and local roads and properties. The flood waters were as high as 3-5 feet and caused serious damage to property and loss of productivity to local industries. I invited property owners, and officials representing two railroad companies, local businesses, the city, the county, and the state to a meeting on December 9, 1996 to formulate a plan to ensure that flooding did not continue to occur. Numerous individuals attended that first meeting, and discussions continued at similar sessions for much of the month.

My goal was to agree on a plan before the January 13 opening day of the 1997 legislative session began, when I would need to devote my attention to my duties in Salem. It was a goal that was met with the adoption of a final plan on January 9, 1997. Representatives from ODOT, Wah Chang Albany, Union Pacific Railroad, and Burlington Northern/Santa Fe all agreed to install new or larger culverts on their property to draw more water into the Willamette River when heavy rain flooded Truax Creek. Each pledged to be responsible for its own costs, permits, and construction. I was very proud when, at the conclusion of that final meeting, the representative from the Oregon Department of Transportation congratulated me on solving a thirty-five-year flood problem in a month's time. In 1998, Millersburg Mayor Clayton Wood honored my efforts when he presented me with an engraved water pitcher, which he termed the "Come Hell or High Water Award!"

While I regarded all constituent service requests as very important, I have to admit that I gave extra special attention to requests from veterans. I believe that those who risked their life for the United States have earned a debt of gratitude that can never be repaid. There were many times when I received a call from a veteran who believed he or she had been mistreated by the Oregon Department of Veteran's Affairs, and I would not rest until the situation was corrected.

I was especially honored in 1986 to be the featured speaker at two community Memorial Day services. It was a beautiful ceremony with the laying of wreaths, and tributes from 23 civic organizations. The weather was glorious, and a light breeze blew the American flags, while the sound of "Taps" echoed from the surrounding hills. In my remarks, I told the attendees that I had seen war close up when I lived under Japanese occupation in Shanghai during the Japanese invasion and World War II. I understood what it meant to put your life on the line for what you believed in. I also saw what happened to my father when the Communists took over China and personal freedoms were denied and property seized. I concluded by saying, "Let us grasp with fearless hands the flag so nobly borne before and like those others, plant it always on the battlements of righteousness."

I share this story with you because I hope that you will always remember the debt America owes to our veterans. Whenever you see someone in the uniform of your country, treat them with respect, and thank them for their service. I am also very proud of the role I played in lowering interest rates on home loans to veterans. This occurred when an Albany real estate broker contacted me to express his belief that the Oregon

Department of Veterans Affairs was violating Oregon law, the United States Constitution, and impairing homeowners' existing contractual rights by changing the interest rates on real estate loans that had been transferred once. I wrote to the DVA Director in support of my constituent's concern, and requested an opinion on the matter from the Oregon Attorney General. The Attorney General affirmed my constituent's belief with an opinion on August 2, 1982, that rolled back interest rates for up to 20,000 Oregon veterans.

Just as standing by my principles and standing up for the people of my district frustrated some of my legislative colleagues, it also frustrated some state bureaucrats. During the 1989 legislative session, a memo from the Executive Director of the State Board of Pharmacy stating that "State Senator Mae Yih is not overly bright" was leaked to the press and became public. Some of my colleagues called for the Executive Director's resignation. I did not join the call, and instead just said how surprised I was by the remarks since I had a very good relationship with the pharmacists in my district. Eventually, the executive director was reprimanded by the board, and her salary was reduced by 10% for three months. Probably the best perspective on this incident came from Hasso Hering, the Editor of the Albany Democrat-Herald, who stated in an editorial that "using a written memo to publicly insult someone who had authority over your agency's request for a 10% budget increase made it easy to guess who was not overly bright!" I was also pleased when two constituents sent letters to the Democrat Herald praising me for not being a rubber stamp for government agency budget increases.

As my reputation as a legislator who was willing to go to bat for her constituents increased, so, too, did the number of "interesting" and somewhat humorous requests I received.

For instance, I was once contacted by a woman who complained about the fact that a county road sign provided directions to a church. She believed that the separation of church and state prohibited such a mention. She also took the time to inform me that she was a witch!

Then there was the woman who wrote to me expressing her belief that her fiancée was being held in the state prison longer than other convicts, and she objected to having to undergo a strip search for drugs each time she visited her fiancé in prison. Less than seven months later, I received a letter from the same woman stating that the state parole board was not reviewing her fiance's case in a timely manner and that her fiancé was also not receiving vocational training in the state prison. The interesting part of the second letter was that it involved a different fiancé!

I also received a letter from a woman who had an issue not with two fiances, but with two possible fathers. Apparently, she did not know which of the two men was the father of her child, and she wanted help from the Child Support Enforcement Division in getting child support from one or both of them!

My job as a state legislator was to provide assistance to my constituents, so I made sure that the proper state agency was aware of all of the above requests. That was better than I could do for the constituent who wrote to ask me why I hadn't answered his last letter—and his letter wasn't signed and included no name or return address!

Perhaps my favorite letter, however, was from the homeless individual who wrote to me in pencil on a post card asking for information on how to obtain rental assistance for low -income citizens. I forwarded him information I received on the subject from the Oregon Housing Authority. Several weeks later I received a response from him, thanking me for the information. His letter was written on a piece of a brown paper bag, and he had taped a nickel to his letter. He wrote, "Enclosed is a little money for your campaign this fall. Best wishes and I will vote for you." It was the best campaign contribution I ever received!

If there was one incident that cemented my reputation as a legislator who would do everything possible for her constituents, it was a two-and-a-half-year property tax reduction battle I waged from 1997 to 2000. In fact, as I look back, it was probably the most challenging and time consuming effort of my public service career. It will take some time to explain the whole matter—and some of it will be on the technical side—but I promise that if you stick with it and read the whole story, you will see your grandmother was very persistent in righting a wrong that was done to my constituents due to a legislative drafting oversight.

It all began in May of 1997 when the voters of Oregon passed Ballot Measure #50 (Ballot Measure #50 had been drafted by the legislature to make another ballot measure passed in 1996 workable). Voters were told that passage of this "Cut and Cap" measure would result in reducing the total of all taxing district levies in the state by 17% from the 1995 levels, and roll back the maximum assessed value of property in the state for the 1997-98 tax year to 90% of the property's real market value in the 1995-96 tax year. It also limited any future increase in maximum assessed value to 3% per year. However, when Linn County property owners began to receive their tax bills in the mail in late 1997 they were shocked to see that their property taxes had actually *increased.* I quickly received many irate phone calls and letters from constituents detailing increases in their property taxes ranging from .5% to a whopping 59.15%. They wondered how this could happen, given the passage of Ballot Measure #50. Upon researching the issue, I found that property taxes across Oregon declined by an average of 8%, while the average Linn County property tax bill increased by 1.4%.

I contacted the Department of Revenue, the Legislative Revenue Office, and the Legislative Counsel Office to ask for an explanation. They replied that during the election in May 1997, Linn County voters had also approved a temporary property tax levy to fund the office of the Linn County Sheriff. This levy was intended to replace one that expired, but Measure 50 calculated temporary local option taxes in such a way that it was actually *added* to the expiring levy, resulting in counting the replacement portion twice. Taxpayers were "paying double for the county law levy—once for the old expired law levy, and again for the newly approved levy. To make matters worse, the old expired law levy, less 10%, was distributed to all taxing districts in 1997. This allowed tax rates for all other taxing districts in Linn County to be apportioned a higher share than expected if the sheriff's levy had been permanent. A similar levy also passed in 1997 in the city of Sweet Home, further increasing taxes in that community. The bottom line was that Linn County residents (and resident of Deschutes County in central Oregon, where a similar situation occurred) were being hit with higher property taxes that flew in the face of promises that had been made in Measure 50.

I immediately began to look for a way to fix the totally unfair and unintended increase. Many suggested that Linn County taxing districts simply refund the unexpected tax windfall, but after studying the issue, we were advised that could not be done legally. I then joined with other area legislators in suggesting that the legislature could quickly meet in a one-day special session and pass a bill that would retroactively fix the law and bring Linn and Deschutes counties in compliance with the rest of the state. Legislative leaders told us that they were reluctant to call a special session, as they were concerned the session might get sidetracked by legislators demanding votes on a whole series of controversial issues.

Faced with that news, and believing that waiting two years for the Legislature to pass corrective legislation would be too long and unfair to my constituents, I met with officials of the Department of Revenue, Legislative Revenue and Legislative Counsel to find a way out of the mess. It was suggested that the 61 taxing districts in Linn County could be asked to not spend the unexpected revenue they would be receiving due to the drafting oversight in Measure 50, and to return it to the taxpayers in the form of lower tax levies in the fall of 1998. Linn County Assessor Mark Noaks concurred and promised to help coordinate the effort.

I immediately mailed letters to 42 taxing districts in Linn County (19 others only levied less than $90 in taxes, so I did not contact them), and urged that they pass resolutions to take such an action within 30 days, thereby correcting the mistake of the drafting oversight. I attached letters from the Department of Revenue and Legislative Counsel, explaining the problems, and a letter from the Legislative Revenue Office stating the estimated revenue each Linn County taxing district would lose if part of the Linn County law levy and the City of Sweet Home levy were treated as replacement levies. I also predicted that the result of their collective actions would comply with the voters' wishes under Measure 50 in property tax reduction and maintain faith and credibility with citizens of Linn County,

Local newspaper Albany Democrat-Herald editor, Hasso Hering, who has long been known for his astute observations and in-depth knowledge of local and state issues, attended the January Interim Joint Legislative Revenue Committee meeting, and commented about the complex Measure 50 mix-up, saying "Don't blame legislators for another screw-up. Voter initiatives have made the property tax so convoluted that no human being with a normal life can be aware of all its angles." He also wrote that "all the talk about the property tax and Measure 50 must have made people dizzy, inducing irreversible comas." I totally agreed with his comments, and was grateful that my college and graduate school training in economics and accounting allowed me to follow the complex process and understand the problems.

To their credit, the Linn County Board of Commissioners and the Linn County Sheriff endorsed my plan, and the commissioners announced that they would cut county taxes by $1 million in the fall to make up for the unanticipated revenue. I congratulated the commissioners and pledged to introduce legislation in the 1999 session that would permanently fix the problem.

Many of the other taxing districts—which included cities, schools, education service districts, community colleges, and fire and protection districts—did not quickly respond to my letter and proposal. Concerned that they might simply keep and spend the unanticipated and undeserved revenue, I resolved to spend the next sixteen days attending the next regular meetings of twelve district boards and councils, so I could personally ask them to comply with my proposal to correct the drafting oversight and answer their questions. I decided to pay for an advertisement in the local newspaper listing the times and dates of the meetings I would be attending, and asked concerned citizens to attend and support my plan.

When I attended the meetings, I brought with me resolutions for the districts' consideration and adoption that were drafted by Legislative Revenue officers in consultation with the Department of Revenue and Legislative Counsel, and with all the amounts to be reduced verified by Mark Noakes, the Linn County Assessor.

I especially remember the Saturday morning when I called Mark at his home to make sure his office verified an amount I needed for the school board meeting I was attending the following Monday evening. He politely told me that he was on his way out of his door to go fishing and to please call back Monday morning for the correct amount. I found out later that he was an avid fisherman and a beautiful Saturday was not to be wasted in legislative paperwork!

I would eventually end up attending approximately 30 board meetings of various taxing districts in a six-month period. Monday evenings were the most popular time for such meetings, and there were quite a few Mondays where I would dash from community to community attending as many as two or three meetings.

I was delighted that the Albany School Board agreed with my recommendation that they adopt a lower tax rate for the next two years. The Albany School Board Chairman, Forrest Reid, said, "We feel it is appropriate that we not benefit by the Measure 50 oversight."

I had to attend Albany City Council meetings four times before they agreed to not levy the $1.3 million of the city's allowed property tax, returning the unanticipated revenue in the face of an upcoming road maintenance levy that fall. It took Councilman Jim Linhart's vote by speakerphone from Idaho to pass the city's 1998-99 budget during the Albany City Council's June meeting. Without Linhart's participation, the vote would have been 3-2, and the proposed budget would have failed. The city charter required at least four "yes" votes for something to pass. I was pleased with the passage of the reduced levy to help correct the Measure 50 glitch, and sighed a big sigh of relief at such a tight vote. I believe my practice of contacting managers and board members before meetings to answer questions and clarify issues helped. I always believed that communication is the best way to solve problems.

I didn't do as well with the Linn-Benton and Lincoln Education Service District Board, meeting four times with them without winning any tax rate adjustment. I attended the Linn-Benton Community College Board three times and they voted to lower their tax rate for only one year to compensate for the over collection. School districts were more cooperative in lowering their rates to compensate for the Measure 50 glitch, since they were being compensated by law in state school support funds for any loss in revenue.

I received words of encouragement from many constituents who were grateful for my efforts to ensure that they were not unfairly taxed. These words kept me going in the face of repeated criticism from two local newspapers, the Albany Democrat Herald and the Brownsville Times. The Democrat Herald suggested that the next legislature was not likely to make any changes to the permanent tax rates; that the city was already receiving less tax revenue due to delinquent payments, and that I was only urging the correction of rates for political expediency. The Times editorial argued that the local government districts were already facing enough budget cuts. Some members of the taxing district boards also were hostile to my plea, saying that they had already spent the money or that it was all the fault of the legislature and that I was asking blood to be spilled.

In the end, 14 taxing districts complied with my recommendation, and my efforts in persuading boards and councils to reduce property taxes in Linn County resulted in a total savings of approximately $7.3 million for taxpayers—a little short of my goal of $9 million in savings.

All the meetings I attended and all the work I did in 1998 was just the first step in my efforts to ensure that the intent of the voters in approving Measure 50 was honored. My top priority in the 1999 legislative session was the passage of two measures to provide a permanent "fix" to the issue.

The first measure—SB 123—directed the Department of Revenue to recalculate and reduce the permanent tax rates of local governments in Linn and Deschutes Counties, and the city of Sweet Home, correcting the calculation of the temporary law enforcement tax levies approved in May of 1997.

The second—SJR 1—placed a proposed Constitutional Amendment on the May 2000 ballot which would adjust the permanent tax rates of Linn and Deschutes Counties, as well as the City of Sweet Home, further decreasing property taxes in those areas.

I joined with Senator Neil Bryant from Deschutes County in devoting a great deal of time shepherding these bills through the House and Senate Revenue Committees and onto the floor of both chambers, where they were unanimously passed. The Governor's signature on SB 123 completed the process. (Constitutional amendment SJR 1 did not require the Governor's signature, because it was to go to the voters for their approval in 2000.).

We were successful with the bills in spite of opposition from several cities and fire districts in Linn County. The Legislative Revenue Office said that if I had not been successful in convincing so many districts to not spend the unanticipated revenue and to return the collected taxes, the corrective measures would not have passed, due to the budget shock such a correction would cause. The long-term benefit of passage of SB 123 has been a permanent and uniform reduction of tax rates. As of 2015, the time of this writing, SB 123 has saved Linn County taxpayers $5 million a year for 18 consecutive years since 1997, for a total savings of $90 million so far—and that doesn't count the additional savings that have resulted from an annual property assessment growth rate of 3%.

Even after my legislative success, I knew that my job wasn't finished. If Linn County property taxes were to be reduced to the levels promised by Measure 50, then Oregon voters would need to pass SJR 1, the Constitutional Amendment—which was designated as Measure #77—in the May 2000 primary election. I became convinced that passage might be difficult when the Oregon Attorney General announced that the official explanation of the measure—which is written on the ballot—would read "Amends constitution: Increase certain local taxing districts' permanent property tax rate limits."

While this explanation was technically true, it was also very confusing, as the increase in the permanent rate was offset by a corresponding decrease in local option taxes. The replacement portion of the law enforcement levy, when added to the county's permanent rate, would result in stability in funding, and a further net tax decrease for citizens in Linn and Deschutes Counties and the city of Sweet Home. Senator Neil Bryan and I contacted the Attorney General to express our concern that the ballot measure title was misleading. Eventually, the Attorney General changed the ballot title to read "Amends constitution: Makes certain local taxing districts' temporary property tax authority permanent."

Senator Bryant and I decided to accept this new ballot title, and to make sure that the material included in the Voters' Pamphlet that was mailed to all Oregon voters would clearly explain that Measure 77 was not a tax increase, rather it was a transfer and net tax decrease in Deschutes and Linn Counties, and the city of Sweet Home. In retrospect, I wish we had not accepted this title, and had insisted on a ballot title that made it clear to the voters that Measure 77 corrected a Measure 50 drafting error and that it would result in stability and equal treatment of the law enforcement levy in Linn and Deschutes counties and a net tax decrease. We submitted a written explanation to Measure 77 for the statewide Voters' Pamphlet, purchased advertisements in newspapers in Portland, Salem, and Eugene, visited five editorial boards, and wrote letters to the editor of newspapers across the state, urging a yes vote.

We said: "This will bring fairness to the property tax system, equity in the treatment of local levies for essential services and, more importantly, help restore faith and credibility in local and state governments." In April 2000, Albany Democrat-Herald editor Hasso Herring wrote, "Enact 77: Don't Read It," correctly stating, "If Oregon voters read the text of Ballot Measure 77…they will get dizzy, and headaches may ensue. So for the sake of their physical and mental health, they are hereby referred instead to the statement in support of the measure submitted by Linn County Sheriff Dave Burright. In the Voters' Pamphlet, Burright explains that because of a "complicated quirk" (understatement of the year) in Ballot Measure 50, the property tax lid approved in 1997, taxes in Sweet Home and Linn and Deschutes Counties went up instead of going down. It took legislative action in 1999 to fix this and now it also takes a clarification in the language that Measure 50 placed in the Constitution. And for that, voter approval is required. Voters should say yes. For good measure, check the explanatory statement provided by Senator Mae Yih and others. But for heaven's sake, *do not clap your eyes on the text itself. It would drive you mad."*

An editorial in the Sweet Home newspaper agreed, stating "Like Oregon's increasingly Byzantine property tax system, state ballot measure 77 seems designed to give voters mental motion sickness. In fact, readers with a low tolerance for stultifying detail might want to stop reading now and simply take it on faith that this is a measure worth supporting or pop an Advil here if you want to read on about the problem…"

Unfortunately, despite all Senator Bryant's and my efforts, on May 17, 2000, Measure 77 went down to defeat. Hasso Hering would comment in the Albany Democrat-Herald that "The majority of voters who defeated Ballot Measure 77 cast a new shadow over Oregon's system of direct legislation. By killing a harmless measure to fix a technical defect in a previous tax measure, a defect that affects only three jurisdictions, including Deschutes County, Linn County and Sweet Home, they showed that the system does not work. The problem was clear enough. Property taxes in the affected jurisdictions in 1997 did not fall as much as promised. But the provisions that caused the problem were exceedingly technical. The solution was technical as well. The language of the ballot title was utterly incomprehensible. What this suggests is this: If there is a technical problem in the state constitution because the voters helped put it there, it remains forever, because the electorate is unlikely to understand enough of it to make repairs."

I was interviewed by the press after the defeat of Ballot Measure 77, and said that we should try to write a simpler and clearer ballot title and explanation and try again to pass it, as it would bring fairness to the property tax system, equity in the treatment of local levies for essential services, and provide law enforcement a more stable funding base. However, during the 2001 legislative session, the Linn County Sheriff and County Commissioners did not request that I make another attempt.

Priority #2: Restraining the size and spending of government, and promoting growth and economic development

My philosophy can be summed up in words often credited to Thomas Jefferson: "The best government is that which governs the least." This means that government needed to not become too large and intrusive, and to spend tax dollars wisely and effectively. Also, if taxes are kept low, people will have more money to spend on their own projects and business will have more money to spend on expansion and growth. People can spend their own money much more efficiently than government can. Lower taxes keep existing businesses competitive and thriving. It also attracts new businesses and industries, which leads to greater employment and revenue.

My efforts to keep taxes and government spending in line were even more important in times of economic recession—and, thanks in large parts to government policies that devastated our forest products industry—Oregon spent much of the 1980's in recession. For example, during the 1981 legislative session, we were faced with the fact that the total state revenue was barely above the 1979 level, and that a $450 million budget shortfall was projected. Governor Vic Atiyeh proposed to fix this shortfall by cutting programs by $200 million and raising taxes by $250 million.

According to basic economic principles I learned in college the last thing you should do during a recession is to raise taxes. Instead, I introduced legislation that would freeze expenditures at 1979 levels, therefore requiring no tax increases. After seven months of wrangling, the Governor, Senate, and House agreed on a compromise budget that included an increase in the cigarette tax, elimination of the weatherization tax credit, some additional tinkering with the tax code, but no actual income tax increase. I voted against the compromise package, saying that instead of a "patch-up" approach, the budget deficit demanded that we be serious about setting priorities, and that we cut obsolete programs and duplicative spending. Government should do what families and private businesses do. When there is not enough money, you tighten your belt, live within your means, and do what is essential. My warning was proved correct when the legislature had to return to special session in January 1982 to find more money to cover a deficit that continued to grow.

The worsening recession was on top of the agenda when the 1983 legislative session—my first in the State Senate—began that January. My proposal again was that government spending should be frozen. The Governor's proposal increases state spending by an amazing 15% from the previous biennium—an increase greater than the growth rates in population, consumer price index, and personal income. The proposed spending increase was on top of the fact that Oregon's property taxes had increased by 41% during the previous two years. I ended up as the only Democrat in the Senate to oppose a budget balancing revenue package containing $437 million in tax increases.

During the 1983 session there were countless proposals to increase taxes and fees, including: 3 different income tax plans, 5 different lottery proposals, 3 different sales tax proposals, 2 proposed new gas taxes, a bill for increased corporate taxes, a bill to allow counties to impose their own taxes on vehicles, a tax on fraternal orders like the Elks and the Eagles that would remove their property tax exemption.

I stood fast on my conviction that there should be no increases in taxes—especially during the worst recession Oregon had faced in 50 years. I advocated freezing spending or reducing it by 4% to stay within the state's predicted revenue. However, despite good public support at the committee hearing of my "freeze the budget" proposal, only one other legislator signed on as a co-sponsor, and the bill did not move out of committee.

Without a freeze, Oregon's budget continued to increase. The increased spending was funded by—what else—increased taxes. By the mid 1980's, Oregon ranked 14th out of the 50 states in terms of total state and local taxes as a percentage of income. In addition, Oregon's property taxes skyrocketed nearly 50% in a four-year period. A constituent pointed out to me that property taxes on a $140,000 home in Seattle, Washington were about $1,000. Property taxes for that same value home in Albany were $3,000-3,500. Oregon's reputation as a high tax state came with a price—other lower-tax states were outdoing Oregon when it came to attracting new businesses and jobs. In hopes of turning the situation around, in 1986 I testified before the Joint Legislative Interim Committee on Revenue and School Finance in favor of my proposal to cut state income taxes 5% annually for four years—a total of a 20% cut. I also proposed that a special review committee be empowered to look for spending cuts. Had my proposal been adopted, I believe Oregon would have experienced a strong economic recovery, as the state would have been much more attractive to many businesses. Unfortunately, Oregon continued down a high-tax and high-spending path, and Oregon continued to experience financial difficulties for much of the next decade.

In the early 1990's, Oregon's economy was in full recession mode. In November 1990, Oregon voters expressed their concern about rapid increases in the property tax by passing Ballot Measure #5, which mandated reducing property taxes over a six year period to 1.5% of the property's value. The same election, voters also elected Democrat Barbara Roberts as Oregon's first woman governor. The 1991 legislative session was dominated by the fact that by 1995 the state would have to find $2.6 billion dollars in additional K-12 school funding, to make up for the money Oregon's school districts would lose (as they were largely funded by the property tax) because of the passage of Measure #5. As the session began, Governor Roberts submitted a budget that would find the $630 million needed for K-12 for the biennium by cutting most other government programs—including higher education— by 10 to 12%. Instead of cutting budget, some legislators were advocating we find the $630 million by implementing a sales tax, or by lifting the statutory state spending limit, which tied state spending to personal income growth. I stated that I opposed any attempt to raise taxes or shift the tax burden. Instead, in passing Measure #5, Oregonians made clear they wanted to see a more efficient state government.

As a member of the Education Subcommittee of the Joint Ways and Means Committee I identified several areas for potential savings. For instance, I asked the Chancellor of Higher Education to comment on a study published in the *Barometer,* the campus newspaper of Oregon State University, that revealed that Oregon State University and the University of Oregon spent more money per student on administrators than any other university in the Pacific 10 conference. OSU's cost per student was $35.41 and University of Oregon's was $31.65—both more than double that of Arizona State University's cost per student of $15.28! As a result of my efforts, a performance audit of higher education administrative costs was authorized.

I also introduced legislation to close the University of Oregon Law School in 1993. My reasoning was that Oregon already had two law schools at private universities in Salem and Portland, and both those law schools had not been threatened with loss of accreditation by the American Bar Association, as had the University of Oregon Law School. Additionally, states of similar size as Oregon, such as Iowa, Wisconsin, and Mississippi were getting by with two law schools each. California, with a population of 29 million, had 16 law schools, amounting to two law schools for every 3.6 million residents. Alaska and Nevada had no law school at all. One-fourth of the students at the University of Oregon Law School were from out of state and were not Oregonians. At a time where every dollar mattered, the state could save $3-4 million every two years by shutting down the law school—even after funding 100 scholarships of $6,500 each for qualified Oregon students to attend the two private law schools. My proposal complied with the wishes of the voters who passed Ballot Measure #5. I believed my proposal was a "win-win," as it cut duplication, reduced costs, and increased efficiency. However, it did not even receive a hearing, either in the Judiciary Committee or the Ways and Means Subcommittee on Education. I did ask higher education officials for an annual report listing the University of Oregon Environmental Law Clinic clients.

The clinic had often represented environmental groups that sued to block the harvest of old growth timber. The clinic also had appealed a new water discharge rate for Pope and Talbot, the Halsey pulp mill. The appeal was later rejected when the Willamette River study was completed and the toxins from the mill's water discharge level was found at an extremely low level.

In order to cut the budget by $630 million to comply with Measure #5's reduction of property taxes, I proposed reducing school expenditures by $315 million and reducing other state agency budgets by $315 million. Instead, the legislature increased basic school support by 5.5%. This was completely opposite to what the people demanded.

As the economy continued to sputter, Governor Roberts called for a one-day special session in 1992, in hopes the legislature would refer to Oregon voters her one-billion dollar tax package implementing a 3.5% sales tax on goods while partially lowering personal income taxes.

I made it very clear from the beginning that the Governor's proposal would not have my support. Increasing taxes during a recession would only further harm the economy and make it tougher for citizens and businesses to survive. I also stated my belief that a sales tax is a regressive tax, as the people who could afford it the least got taxed the most. The best way to improve the state's economy was to reduce wasteful government spending, lower taxes, and eliminate excessive regulations on business. These actions would promote economic development opportunities and create jobs.

I didn't have to look very hard to find examples of the high tax burden on Oregonians. In fact, *Money* Magazine reported in the spring of 1992 that Oregon had the 2nd highest tax burden in the country—trailing only New York. And when it came to government waste and overspending, the case was made when it was revealed that carpet for a newly constructed State Archive building cost $127 a yard, and light fixtures for the building were $5,000 each. This was all the proof needed to make the point that if the state government needed more money, then they should eliminate wasteful spending before they asked the public for more tax dollars.

The chaotic 1992 special session ended up as a total fiasco. The session convened on July 1, and Governor Roberts' proposed tax increase ballot measure was first debated by the House of Representatives, as the Oregon Constitution provided that revenue-raising measures must originate in the House. The Republican-controlled House quickly defeated the Governor's plan 33-26 and then voted to adjourn the session. The Democrat-controlled Senate then voted 16-10 (I voted "no") to approve the Governor's plan. The Republican Senators objected to the vote saying that tax proposals could not legally start in the Senate. The vote was ruled proper, as the Constitution stated that either the House or the Senate could originate a proposed Constitutional amendment. The Governor's plan did include asking the voters to amend the Constitution to impose a sales tax and other tax changes.

Senate President John Kitzhaber did not want to vote for the Governor's plan, as after the vote in the House, he helped to persuade legislative leaders of both parties to sign a statement pledging to begin new legislative efforts to resolve the state's budget problem. Since the vast majority of his caucus supported the plan, he felt he had to provide the needed 16th vote. Before voting for it, however, he sent an aide to ask me to provide the 16th vote, so he could vote against it. I immediately rejected the request. Normally, if the Senate President asked for something, I would try to oblige—but I could not oblige if it violated my principle of doing what is right.

The special session eventually adjourned without taking final action on the Governor's proposal. It was an embarrassing defeat for the Governor, who should not have called the special session without having legislative involvement and a commitment from enough legislators to pass her plan.

Going into the November 1992 election, there were 20 Democrats and 10 Republicans in the State Senate. After the election, the 67th Oregon Legislature that would convene in January 1993 would feature a Senate with 16 Democrats and 14 Republicans. A number of Democrat state senators who voted for the sales tax during the Governor's ill fated special session met resounding defeats.

As planning began for the 1993 session, I hosted a "no tax increase summit" in Albany. I asked fourteen participants from varying backgrounds to present their views on how the 1993 legislature could regulate spending and make cuts that would enable the state to get through the 1993-1995 biennium without raising taxes or cutting essential services.

In addition to the fourteen invited panelists, thirty-four persons attended the summit on a windy, rainy evening. Among the common sense suggestions offered by the panelists and those in the audience: Cut from the top, don't eliminate front-line services; consolidate jobs and form agency partnerships to eliminate duplication of services; curtail administrative rules that burden schools, local governments, and businesses; contract out services that can be provided more efficiently by private firms; and getting a handle on too generous government pensions.

As I listened to the testimony at my anti-tax summit, I knew that the nearly evenly-divided Senate created an opportunity to move Oregon in much-needed new direction.

It takes 16 votes to accomplish anything in the Senate, including to pass legislation and to elect the Senate President. The Democrat caucus had decided by majority vote that Senator Bill Bradbury would be their choice for Senate President. Since the 14 Republicans were voting for their leader, Senator Gene Timms, Bradbury could not be President without my vote. I told my caucus that in order for me to vote for Bradbury, I would have to be named as Co-Chair of the Joint Ways and Means Committee, which would put me in the strongest position possible to control state government spending and to ensure that the state would live within existing revenues without increasing taxes. Oregon voters had approved Ballot Measure #5, which placed a strict limit on property taxes, sending a message that they did not want increased taxes. As a veteran of the Ways and Means Committee, I believed that my proposal made sense: to cut 3% from current government spending and to freeze it at that level for two years.

When Senator Bradbury refused my request, I refused to give him my vote, and when the Senate convened on Monday, January 11, I held my ground, voting for myself for Senate President on eleven separate ballots for nearly a week, while 15 other Democrats voted for Bradbury and the 14 Republicans voted for Timms.

During the deadlock, some of my Democrat colleagues criticized me, saying that my holdout was costing taxpayers $29,000 a day for a session that was accomplishing nothing. I responded in a speech on the Senate floor, saying that "This is probably the most important session in the last twenty years. As the state and its citizens face a fiscal crisis, my constituents have asked me to do everything I can to properly represent them. They tell me to reduce their tax burden, to cut government spending, to live within our revenue and improve Oregon's economy. To do this we need to select the right leaders —leaders who will endeavor to follow the people's mandate. It may take us a few days to get organized, but once we select our leaders and set the right course, we will be able to save taxpayers as much as $1.2 billion in taxes that we do not need to raise. We need to take some time to make sure that we do not send out hundreds of millions of dollars in tax proposals that the people do not want. If we fail and have to call a special session to come back and rewrite the budget, it will cost taxpayers far more money than what we are spending the first few days it takes us to set the right course. Let us have patience and vision, so we can work together to carry out the mandate of the people of Oregon."

I was proud that my weeklong hold-out led to my receiving countless bouquets of flowers, faxes and phone calls from citizens all over the state who were supportive of my position. When asked if I was worried that my stance might lead to my fellow Democrats totally freezing me out of any legislative position, I said, "I think it's worth taking the risk. People are tired of politicians doing their own thing and not listening to the people. It's not time for business as usual. It's important that I stand up for my convictions that this is what people want. We need to have a change, and listen to the taxpayers about government fiscal responsibility and accountability."

On the morning of Friday, January 15, the Democrat Party Chairman of Linn County called me to say that the Democrat caucus has convinced one Republican Senator to break ranks and to give Bradbury the 16th vote he needed. His advice was that if Bradbury was going to be elected without my vote, then I could achieve more for my district if I provided the 16th vote. I called Roger Reid, who had been my campaign chairman in all my legislative races, and he gave me the same advice. Before voting for Bradbury, however, I received a guarantee that I would be named as Chairman of the Ways and Means Subcommittee on General Government, a post that would allow me to continue to be a real watchdog on government spending. I also was elected as Senate President Pro Tempore—the first woman in Oregon history to hold the position—which meant that I would be the presiding officer of the Senate in the absence of the Senate President. In that position, I was also entitled to hire an additional staff member—which I refused to do, as I was promoting a 3% cut in government spending and freeze it for two years. (Later in the session I would also announce that I would return the $2 a day increase in the legislator's daily expense allowance. I would also have refused a $103 a month legislative pay raise that had automatically become effective without any legislative action, but was advised by the legislature's legal counsel that there was no way I could be paid less than other state legislators. Therefore, at the end of the year, I donated to various Linn County charities the money I received in the raise. I could not accept the raise with a clear conscience.)

In the days following my hold-out, a number of citizens drove to Albany to ask me to run for governor in 1994. I told them it was out of the question, as I was confident that the Portland liberals who dominated the Democrat hierarchy would not support me. In retrospect, I should have told them that I would like to take some time to think about their proposal. Perhaps there would have been support for a gubernatorial candidate with a fiscally conservative, live within the state's income philosophy, and a low tax, less unnecessary regulation and stronger economic development policy.

I was very proud of the editorial that ran in the Albany Democrat Herald, stating that "Senator Yih asserted herself in a way powerful enough to assure that her views on state spending—she's for less rather than more—will continue to be heard. She served powerful notice which could not be missed, that without her vote the Senate majority might as well be a minority. Without her, Democrats can't pass anything on a party-line vote. Even though she gave in, she may not have lost."

The tense and difficult January beginning of the 1993 session was repeated in August, as the record 207-day session—the longest in state history—lurched to a conclusion. There was a rumor that Senate President Bradbury might be resigning to accept an appointment with the new Clinton Administration in Washington, D.C. Under the rules of the Senate, if no new Senate President was elected before Bradbury's resignation, then the Senate President Pro Tem would step into the job. Word then reached me that some of the democrat state senators wanted to elect a "senate president-in-waiting" before adjournment, so that the President Pro Tem wouldn't assume that position.

I resented this manipulation of the system, seeing it as an affront to the honor and integrity of the rules of the senate. I went to see Senator Gene Timms and Senate Republican leader Gordon Smith and we reached an agreement that no Republican would break ranks and support any election to install a Senate President-in-waiting before adjournment. Further, I would support an increase in proportional representation for the Republicans on the powerful Emergency Board, which was authorized to make government spending decisions during the interim between the legislative sessions. Senate President Bradbury thought he could sabotage our agreement by telling Senator Smith that he would agree to increase Republican representation on the Emergency Board, but that he would not appoint me. Senator Smith refused, saying that they would "stick with Mae until hell freeze over," and would not agree to adjournment unless I was included in the appointments to the Emergency Board. Faced with our united strength, Bradbury gave in, and the Senate Republicans and I got everything we asked for. Bradbury never did receive an appointment to the Clinton Administration.

The role I played at the beginning and end of the 1993 legislative session led to my receiving increased attention from members of the media from outside my legislative district. In 1994, the state's major newspaper, *The Oregonian*, published a profile of me. It was entitled "The Queen of Albany," and focused on my dedication to constituent service. The article also quoted a former state senator who believed that working for my constituents was "trivial" and that I should spend more time becoming a "player" on major legislative issues. I responded by stating "I don't think its trivial, if you don't represent your people and take care of their problems, what's so good about passing laws that may or may not help them?" My statement was vindicated by the words of a retired Oregon State Police lieutenant whom I helped with a retirement benefit issue. "She's done a great deal for an awful lot of people," he said. "It doesn't make a difference to Mae…you can be a nobody."

The article led to my receiving many calls and letters of support and encouragement. Speaker of the Oregon House of Representatives Larry Campbell sent me a note saying, "Not only are you the Queen of Albany, but some of us would say you're the "Queen of the Senate!" The letter that meant the most to me was from my son, Daniel, who wrote a letter to the editor of the Oregonian after the 1994 election responding to the criticism that working for my constituents was trivial and that I should spend more time becoming a player on major legislative issues, stating how proud my family was of my accomplishments, dedication to solving the problems of my constituents, and the fact that I refused to compromise my positions for political expediency.

Throughout my legislative career I was a strong advocate for legislation and policies that would promote the creation of private sector jobs. One of the best tools in the creation of jobs was the creation of "enterprise zones." The basic concept of enterprise zones is to attract businesses to start or expand operations in economically lagging areas by exempting them from local property taxes for five years, and to provide additional local government regulatory relief. During my years in the legislature, I introduced and advanced legislation ensuring that enterprise zone would be created and expanded. I am proud to report that in 2013 there are currently 63 enterprise zones operating in Oregon—50 of them in rural areas, where jobs are often most needed. Linn County had three of the first ten enterprise zones in Oregon, and a 2002 summary provided by Mel Joy of the Albany-Millersburg Economic Development Corporation concluded that nearly 3,500 Linn County jobs had been created under the enterprise zone program since its creation in 1985.

Along with insisting on wise and cost effective spending, I was also equally vigilant on the need for high quality of government service and respecting the dignity and self-esteem of the citizens we served. My motto has always been working for maximum quality of service with minimum of spending. That is why I was totally shocked and appalled in 2001, when I happened to read a news article about a Lane County welfare recipient who attended a workshop of the State Adult and Family Services Division and received a "tip sheet" of suggestions that included "check the dump and residential and business dumpsters." After reading the article, I delivered remarks on the Senate floor to express dismay. To suggest that low-income Oregonians pick through garbage was wholly unacceptable. I circulated a letter to be sent to the Interim Director of Human Services demanding an investigation into the matter, and all of the 26 other Senators who were present that morning signed onto the letter. Further research in the matter revealed that the dumpster tip sheet had been distributed on four other occasions dating back four years, and that the tip sheet continued to be distributed even after three clients voiced concerns. One client actually took the tip to heart, and was arrested for going through a dumpster. I held up the confirmation of a new Director of the Department of Human Services until I was convinced DHS was taking corrective action to ensure that their 9,700 employees served Oregonians with respect and dedication.

That same 2001 session, I helped lead the successful effort to pass legislation that would actually help welfare recipients and unemployed Oregonians find jobs. This legislation provided $25 million out of the unemployment insurance taxes in funding for an innovative and cost effective program entitled "Jobs Plus," which provided employers with a subsidy to hire and train unskilled employees. Over 65% of the participants in the program found unsubsidized jobs at the end of the program, receiving a paycheck and the satisfaction of self-sufficiency.

Examining the performance of state agencies was a priority of mine during my final legislative session in 2001. After all, at a time of limited resources, we needed to know more than ever how effective state agencies were in carrying out their goals, serving our citizens, and achieving the results they are responsible to achieve with the funding the legislature provided. I assisted in writing performance and outcome measures for nine divisions in the Human Resources Department, and several other agencies, including the Employment Department, the Housing Department, the Department of Transportation, and the Board of Nursing.

The performance of the Department of Transportation was a special concern of mine. In the 2000 election, Oregon voters overwhelmingly defeated a ballot measure that would have raised Oregon's gas tax from 24 cents a gallon to 29 cents a gallon.

Gas tax receipts are used to fund highway repairs. Hoping to accomplish in the legislature what they couldn't at the ballot box, several legislators proposed legislation mandating the Motor Vehicles Department to increase car title fees from $10 to $30, and heavy truck title fees from $10 to $90, with the additional revenue to be used for highway repairs.

One of the reasons the gas tax increase had been defeated was that the public believed that the Department of Transportation was a wasteful bureaucracy, and that they spent too much money on administration and other unneeded expenses, and not enough on asphalt and repair crews. I spoke against and voted against the title fee increase package, stating that to add a "profit" of $20 to each car title fee and $80 to each truck title fee to generate revenue for road and bridge repair was contrary to our principle of not charging more than what it cost to carry out our programs and Oregon's tradition of financing highways according to the principle of cost responsibility. I also said that the Transportation Department had not demonstrated a sufficient increase in efficiency in its performance, and before we increased funding for more programs, they needed to show us clear evidence of achievements in efficiency savings.

I pointed out that a good model for ODOT's divisions could be found in their Motor Carrier Services Division, which was able to reduce its workforce by 64 employees (19% of workforce), all the while continuing to provide all of its services. The Division accomplished this through employees absorbing increases in their workload while maintaining quality service delivery. They took full advantage of new technology, pioneering the use of credit card technologies to provide a payment alternative for the public, and also made it possible for the greater use of electronic transactions. I believed that these kinds of farsighted achievements could and should be utilized in other departmental branches, and could translate to millions of dollars of existing ODOT resources that could be redirected to preservation, bridge and modernization projects.

Near the end of the 2001 session, as a member of the Ways and Means Subcommittee on Transportation and Economic Development, I carried the Transportation Department budget for the Senate's approval. I distributed a one- page performance measure to Senators, and informed them that ODOT was falling behind in the percentage of roads in fair condition, and the percentage of bridges with posted load limits. I advocated that ODOT needed to make much needed improvements. I also said that through creative use of advanced technologies, ODOT should be able to reduce their administration, paperwork, and free up more dollars for needed highway projects. The time was coming when ODOT would need to have new funding to meet the growing needs of highway operations. I concluded by stating that ODOT needed to demonstrate that, through its own internal initiatives and efficiencies savings, it could increase the preservation, bridge and modernization programs by 10%. When this was accomplished, a new funding source could be sought.

My father and my mother in 1926. The values that instilled in me have guided my life.

*My brother Jim and I enjoyed riding horses in 1947. Jim was wearing
an honorary volunteer firefighter's uniform.*

*I was privileged to grow up in our family's beautiful house in Shanghai
and to use our new 1946 Chevrolet.*

My graduation photo from MccTyre Girls High School in Shanghai in 1946.
I am the first person on the left in the second row from the front.

Graduation day at Barnard Women's College
of Columbia University in New York in June 1951.

My wedding day June 7, 1953. Stephen and I are joined in the photograph
by my mother, and my two brothers, Tom and Jim.

Donald and a flock of roosters—part
of an Easter 1957 present gone awry.

Donald, age 11 and Daniel, age 7
taking care of our horses in 1966.

I am joined by students at Clover Ridge Elementary School during my 1976 campaign for the House of Representatives.

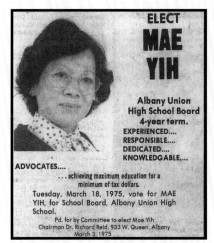

A newspaper advertisement during my campaign for the Albany Union High School Board. Achieving maximum education for a minimum of tax dollars was my guiding principle throughout my community service and legislative career.

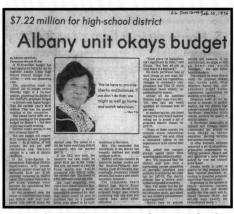

Standing up for my principles as a school board member led to the Democrat party recruiting me to run for the Oregon State Legislature.

*Campaigning for the legislature
involved lots of phone calls and
knocking on countless doors.*

*A citizen's phone call and concern
led me to help save Oregon's
historic covered bridges in 1989.*

Cutting the ribbon on the reconstruction of the historic Cascadia Bridge in April 1994.

*Albany Police Chief Pat Merina and Lt. Wayne Hyde testify
on the importance of adolescent drug and alcohol treatment
in 1990. The Albany attorney Paul Kuebrich is on my right.*

Governor to sign Linn County tax adjustment bill

BY HASSO HERING
Albany Democrat-Herald

Gov. John Kitzhaber has no objections to a bill lowering Linn County property tax rates and will sign it, his press spokesman said today.

The statement came this morning from Bob Applegate, the governor's press secretary.

Both the state Senate and House have passed, without a single dissenting vote, Senate Bill 123 to fix a problem with the way Ballot Measure 50 worked out in Linn and Deschutes counties.

The bill directs the Department of Revenue to lower permanent tax rates in both counties.

In Linn County, the bill will reduce total property taxes an estimated $3.8 million per year below what they otherwise would be.

Whether there is an actual cut in the total depends on several factors including changes in the total property value and whether voters approve any additional local-option taxes.

The bill takes effect in June 2000. It will lower tax rates for those districts that have not already done so on their own.

It allows school districts to levy less than their maximum tax rates again next budget year and be reimbursed for the difference with state funds. Other local governments do not get the reimbursement.

For taxing districts that have not already done so, the bill orders tax rate reductions in 2000-01 big enough to make up for property taxes overcollected during the previous two years.

The total reduction in Linn County in 2000-01 is estimated at $11.2 million, but $7 million of that has not been collected in 12 Linn taxing districts and won't have to be repaid.

Sen. Mae Yih, D-Albany, who cosponsored SB 123, had asked Linn taxing districts to collect less than they legally could.

Applegate said the governor also does not object to SJR 1, a proposed constitutional amendment to fix a related property tax matter in the two counties affected. Because it calls an election the measure does not require the governor's signature.

SJR 1 would shift some of the local-option tax rates for law enforcement into the counties' and the city of Sweet Home's permanent plug-tax rates. In the process the total tax rate would be reduced again, amounting to about $1 million in Linn County.

Ballot Measure 50 passed in May 1997. It was intended to lower property taxes statewide. But in Linn and Deschutes counties, it unexpectedly raised taxes on a majority of properties because of the interplay with local-option levies approved in the same election.

*Sometimes it takes a lot of people to solve
a problem. Here, I convene a meeting of the
Millersburg Flood Control Working Group.*

*Lowering permanent
property taxes for
Linn and
Deschutes County
residents was one
of my most
satisfying legislative
accomplishments.*

*Steve and I had the privilege of meeting President and Mrs. Clinton
and Vice President and Mrs. Gore in Portland, Oregon in September 1996.*

I helped to lead a Linn County delegation of teachers and students to Shitara, Japanin 1996.

I attended a 1987 luncheon for a trade delegation from Fujien Province hosted by Phil Knight, founder and longtime CEO of Nike.

Hugging and feeding a giant panda was a highlight of a visit to China in October 2000.

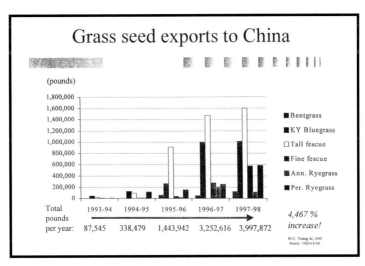

My work to build friendly relationships and economic ties
between Oregon and China was especially successful
for Oregon's grass seed industry.

Sept. 1990

17 SEP 1990

Dear Mrs. Yih,

Thank you very much for your letter regarding low income housing. This information had come forward through my rental agent.

By the way, have you registered with the Selective Service System. You know you should. Enclosed is a list of eligible people.

Also, enclosed is a little money for your campaign this fall. Best wishes, and I will vote for you.

Sincerely,
Joel Witdorg

It may not have been much, but I considered this nickel campaign contribution attached to a brown paper bag to be priceless.

Steve and I surrounded by our family as we celebrate our 50th wedding anniversary in June 2003. From left to right: Stephen, Christopher, Daniel, Nancy, Steve, myself, Donald, Benjamin, Alex and Pam.

*Steve's legacy lives on at West Albany High School through a display
that honors his accomplishments in the specialty metals industry.
Photo by David Patton,* Albany Democrat Herald, *September 2009.*

*Riding the Meg-Lev train to the Shanghai airport in 2008.
The train uses a niobium-alloy, which was first produced
in Albany, Oregon under Steve's leadership.*

During Steve's last trip to China in 2003 we visited Ye Cheng Zhong School, which was founded by his great-grandfather, who is depicted in the statue. After Steve's passing, I donated money to the school for a memorial college scholarship.

My long time campaign chairman Roger Reid and wife Sharon joined Steve and I on a trip to China in September 1999.

Leading a economic and trade delegation visitto China in June 2000. Kate Brown, the current governor of Oregon in on my left.

Surrounded by family following Steve's memorial service in March 2009.

Portland State University published this poster of historic Oregon women. As the first Chinese-American woman elected to a state legislature, I was honored to be included.

Another example of the value of performance measures and budget scrutiny could be seen in the Board of Nursing budget. Part of the Board's request for increased funding was that money would be used to develop electronic options for licensees in the next biennium. They reported that this licensing would help to reduce paperwork and processing time for all licensees. The legislature appropriated the money, but we also wrote in performance measures that required the time it took for a license renewal to be reduced from an average of 8 to an average of 3 days, and for the time it took from successful passage of a nurse certification test to issuance of license to be reduced from 7 to 3 days. This reduction would mean that a nurse waiting for certification to be hired could be hired four days sooner, significantly speeding up employment and helping to resolve the critical nursing shortage. When the Board of Nursing came to the 2003 legislature to justify their budget request, legislators could then review the performance measures to see if they were met.

The bottom line is that throughout my legislative service, I believed that one of the most important things I could do was to do my best to restore faith in government through strict accountability of their spending and performance.

Priority #3: A public school system that focuses on the basics and that wisely uses tax dollars.

One of the first bills I introduced as a new member of the Oregon State House of Representatives in 1977 was a school safety net proposal that would restrain spending and prevent school closures. My proposal was based on my experience as a school board member. I saw first-hand that annual budgets for our schools would always increase, yet their results were decreasing. Oregon's drop-out rate was exceeding the national average and student test scores in reading and writing were drastically declining. As a way to put a brake on ever-increasing state and local spending and property taxes, I proposed legislation that would kick in if a local school levy was defeated two times by voters. In that instance, the school budget would automatically be set at the lower of the budgets of the previous two years.

My proposal and a number of other school funding proposals were blocked in the 1977 session by Senate President Jason Boe, who pushed through his radically different safety net proposal—one that would mandate that if a school budget was defeated twice, then the budget that would be automatically implemented would be the previous year's budget *plus another 6%!* Although President Boe and others heavily lobbied me on this issue, I voted against it because I believed that this would take away local control. It is essential that any funding increase be tied to improvement in the quality of education. The legislature eventually submitted Senate President Boe's proposal to a statewide vote in May 1977, and it was soundly defeated by a 69%-31% margin.

School funding would be a continual issue during my years in the legislature, and every year the argument was the same. Each session, there were those who would say that no matter how much money was appropriated for our public school system, it was not enough. They believed that the only way to improve Oregon's public schools was to spend more money. I disagreed. Instead of ever increasing amounts of money, I suggested that what our schools needed most was stronger courses, an emphasis on values, more efficiency and accountability, and funding that was within our citizens' ability to pay. In fact, in the 1979 session I proposed legislation defining "basic education" as reading, writing, and arithmetic. The legislation also mandated that the state would provide the funding for these educational programs, and that the school district budgets submitted to local voters would, if approved, fund additional programs beyond the basics. The State of Washington operated on a similar system, and their SAT scores were equal to Oregon's, while their cost per student was less, and their income per capita was much higher.

In 1988, I testified before the Governor's Task Force on School Finance. I reminded the Task Force that Oregon's income per capita was ranked 31st in the nation, yet we were ranked 13th highest in terms of cost per student. Simply put, the spending of cost per student was not consistent with the citizen's ability to pay, and we were not getting results for our investment.

I began my testimony with an example that I thought made some very effective points. It was a story about a couple—a man and a wife—who managed a household. The man brought in a nice income, but the wife wanted more, and she told her husband to get a second job to pick up some extra income. The husband then tried to work a little overtime, and he added a part time job. After a while, the wife complained again that she could not make ends meet. So the husband picked up some additional work. He was able to give his wife some more money, but she soon came back to him and said she needed more. The husband finally asked her where all the money went and said that other families were able to get by with the same amount of money he was bringing home without additional part time jobs.

I then compared our school system to the wife in my story. No matter how much money we gave them, they spent it all and wanted more. The legislature was like the good-natured husband, who rarely asked where the money went. I concluded by saying that it was time for the legislature to ask some serious questions. Questions like why on a cost per K-12 student per capita basis, Washington spent 90%, California spent 88%, Texas spent 83%, and Alabama spent 66% of what Oregon spent. I could understand spending more if Oregon students were performing better than students in other states. That, however, was not the case. I requested that the Task Force investigate what other states were doing to achieve high scholastic standards with much less spending, and specifically mentioned New Hampshire, where students SAT scores were higher than those of Oregon students, and where cost per student spending per student was 25% less than ours.

Rather than returning our schools to the basics, many legislators frequently proposed policies that were not helpful to our schools and our students. The most serious of these efforts occurred in 1991 when the legislature passed the "Oregon Educational Act of the 21st Century," which was proposed by House Speaker Vera Katz. Among many provisions of the act was one that replaced the high school diploma with a "certificate of initial mastery," which would be awarded at the end of the 10th grade. After that, students could earn a "certificate of advanced mastery" before entering college or advanced technical training. I was one of only two senators voting against the legislation. Instead of some complex and expensive "reform" requirements, I argued that we could best serve students by giving them strong and challenging courses that make them eager to learn, and by inspiring and motivating them to study hard. My "no" vote was proven correct over the course of time as many school districts in Oregon found the reform legislation to be confusing, bureaucratic and expensive, and the act was totally repealed by the legislature in 2012.

The "charter school" movement that became popular across the country in the 1990's reached the floor of the Oregon State Legislature in the 1999 session. I was a strong supporter of Senate Bill 100, which allowed publicly funded charter schools to be created in Oregon, and provided the crucial 16th vote that allowed the legislation to pass 16-14 in the Senate. In my opinion, charter schools would allow more options for students and their parents, and the competition created by charter schools would encourage public schools to improve their quality and lower costs. As I write this in 2016, over 100 charter schools are operating in Oregon.

Sadly, the expansion of charter schools is about the only victory I can report from my battles with the education bureaucracy. No matter how poorly Oregon students performed, the majority of legislators were unwilling to take the steps necessary to return to the basics and to ensure our students were learning.

For example, in January 2002, I attended a work session with the Albany school superintendent, school board members, and local legislators. The newspaper would later report that I "sounded like a stern teacher quizzing pupils." I asked questions like, "What kind of quality are we getting for our investment?", and "What, for example, is the district's strategy for reducing its dropout rate, which had risen from 6.1 to 6.2%— well above the state average of 5.3%— and why have only 40% of the 10th graders met the state standards in math and just 51% in reading? Most of the meeting was focused on state funding for schools and the February 8 special session of the legislature that was called to erase a projected budget shortfall of more than $700 million. Some legislators were advocating no cuts to funding for public schools. I noted that public school funding was increased by 10% in each of the last two legislative sessions. I also added that "If education doesn't bear its fair share, then other programs will be cut twice as much."

Because the meeting was intended as a discussion between board members and legislators, the superintendent promised to provide written answers addressing all my questions. She did so just a few weeks later, sending seven pages of information and charts. It provided a summary of key points and goals, including commitments to reduce the dropout rate to 2.5% by 2004; improve 10th graders' performance on the state reading and math tests with a goal of 90% of students meeting the standard by 2008; invest the district's $1.4 million school improvement grant in reading programs; invest more than $2 million over seven years in new textbooks; and development by all schools of academic improvement goals focused on reading; I requested that the district monitor its progress in all areas and to keep me apprised of its findings. I also suggested a policy of no social promotion of students. I said it would be helpful to ensure every student learn the basic skills established for each grade level before advancing to the next grade. I said in my response that this gives students an incentive to work hard and also encourages parental involvement and support. My goal was not to be just a critic, but a supporter of improvements and to hold the school district's feet to the fire to make sure students received quality education and taxpayers received a return on our investment.

I would return to the Albany School Board later in 2002 with more data. I shared with them my research that revealed that Oregon's cost per public school student was $186 more than Washington's, even though Oregon's per capita income ranking was much lower. Scores for Oregon students who took the SAT test were similar to Washington's. I also reported that the ratio of administrators to teachers in Oregon was 1 administrator for every 11 teachers—the fourth highest in the nation and well above the 1-16 national average. State support of K-12 education had increased 10% in each of the two previous biennia, and comprised fully 60% of the general fund budget.

I stated that it was clear to me that our children deserved a better education and Oregon taxpayers deserved a better return on their investment. It was also clear that more money did not mean better performance, and we had reached a point where we were funding schools at the expense of adequately funding human services, public safety, natural resources, and other programs.

More than thirteen years after I asked those questions, however, I am disappointed that after promising that 90% of students would meet the reading and math standards by 2008, and spending $3.4 million of school improvement grants and on new textbooks and other promised efforts in improvement, we barely see any improvement in percentages of students meeting state standards in reading and math. A July 2015 report revealed that only 55% of Oregon students were meeting the state standards in reading and only 45% were meeting state standards in math. Most notably and troubling, only 31% of high school juniors were meeting the nationwide proficiency in math.

With this kind of low, pathetic competency in reading and math, what kind of future can we expect for Oregon? How are our youth going to face problems of life, competition for jobs, and various opportunities nationally and globally? How can America assume leadership in science and technology—the driving force behind growth in economy and prosperity?

Policy makers in Salem continue to think the answer is to throw money at the problem. The poor results of the past few decades have proven that more money is not the solution to our education crisis. Growing up in China, I saw first-hand that education does not need to be expensive. What is key to a quality education are involved parents, devoted teachers, and students who are instilled with the values of respect, discipline, hard work, and a love of in-depth learning.

I recalled that during the Japanese occupation and WWII, our all-girls school building and campus were taken by the Japanese soldiers to be used as an army hospital. Our school had to move to a small building in downtown Shanghai and changed to a half-day school system to accommodate education of 6th through 12th grades with approximately 195 students. We had four hours of school each morning or afternoon. I rode my bicycle to school every morning for four hours of courses in Chinese, math, history, science, and English, and came home in the afternoon and did about four hours of assigned homework. In the evening, I practiced brush calligraphy in large and small characters for two hours while making my own ink with an ink stick and an ink stone dish. We were taught English from the fourth grade on. I had nine years of English by the time I came to the United States in 1948 and enrolled in Barnard College as a sophomore. I had my freshman year in St. John's University in Shanghai, China and even with the change of language in text books, I received my BA degree from Barnard in two-and-a-half years instead of three years. This clearly shows that education does not have to be expensive, but it is crucial that students are given strong courses, teaching of discipline and values, and given incentives and support to study hard, learn more, and do their best.

If I were in the legislature today, I would urge my colleagues to seriously consider options such as a voucher plan for elementary and secondary school students, without the current control and approval from the neighboring school districts. Under such a plan, parents could use a state voucher to send their children to a school of their choice, just as veterans are able to choose and pay for a college education through the GI Bill. Such a plan would encourage our public schools to improve if they are to compete for student enrollment. I would also argue that we put an end to "social promotion." If students cannot read, write, and calculate according to the standards set for each grade, then they should not be promoted to the next grade until they do meet those standards. This would help catch their problems early and assist them learning in the elementary grades and not delay until they are frustrated in not learning later, and drop out of school.

John Kennedy once said, "A child mis-educated is a child lost." It is my hope that our state and national leaders will take action to fix our schools before whole generations of children are lost.

Priority #4: A healthy job-producing agriculture and timber economy
One of the most powerful and vocal lobbies in Oregon is the environmental lobby—groups like The Sierra Club and the Oregon League of Conservation Voters. After each session, these groups would release "report cards," that would rate each legislator on how they voted on key environmental bills. I was invariably on the bottom of their scorecards—and I was proud of it. It didn't take me long to conclude that Oregon's legendary United States Senator Mark Hatfield was absolutely correct when he confided to me that the environmentalists had told him their goal was to shut down all timber operations in Oregon. And, thanks to their strategy of filing countless lawsuits anytime it looked like some trees might actually be cut, they were coming very close to reaching their goal. The forest products industry was key to Oregon's economy, providing products in the national and global markets, and thousands upon thousands of good family wage jobs. The industry also understood that if they wanted to succeed they had to be good stewards of the land. I am very proud of the fact that the radical environmental organizations put me on the bottom of their legislative scorecards with a score of a big fat zero. I am also very proud that the forest products businesses and employees put me on the top of their scorecard with a score of 100%.

My advocacy for the industry and the jobs it provided led to my involvement with the Western States Legislative Forestry Task Force, which was comprised of legislators from all the western states. I served as vice chair of the Task Force in 1987, and in January, 1988, I was honored to be elected to serve as Chair. This gave me a stronger position for which to fight for Oregon's interests. As a Task Force chair and member, I made annual visits to Washington, D.C. to advocate our causes to the top officials in the United States Forest Service, Bureau of Land Management, Department of Agriculture, and our Congressional delegation.

Perhaps the most controversial and frustrating issue regarding the timber industry that arose during my time in the Oregon State legislature was the controversy surrounding a bird called the Northern Spotted Owl. I first became involved in the spotted owl controversy in 1986, when United States Forest Service officials took me on a private tour of a forest to show me a spotted owl habitat. I enjoyed the walk in the forest, but never got to see an owl. The USFS biologists even played a tape recording of a spotted owl mating call, in hopes that one would show itself. None did. Then I cupped my hands, sucked in a lungful of air, and let out my best imitation of the mating call! Again, no spotted owl showed.

The issue reached a boiling point in April 1990, when a federally appointed commission, led by U.S. Forest Service biologist Jack Ward Thomas announced that the northern spotted owl had lost about 2/3 of its habitat since 1800, and that more than 3 million acres of previously unrestricted forests—an area nearly as large as the state of Connecticut—needed to be set aside to preserve owl habitat. Such a move would be devastating to the logging industry of Oregon and the Pacific Northwest.

As a state legislator and a member on the Western States Legislative Forestry Task Force, I did everything in my power to fight the assault on the timber industry and to reason that our forests needed to be managed for multiple use to meet the needs of entire communities. My strong belief was that the most important priority of forest management should be economic impact and community stability.

In April, 1990, the Western States Legislative Forestry Task Force (WSLFTF) met in Klamath Falls, Oregon. There, I joined my fellow task force members, which included legislators from Oregon, Washington, Montana, Alaska, California, Idaho, and the Canadian provinces of Alberta and British Columbia, in expressing serious concern that the owl issue threatened our economic and community stability, as it would lead to the loss of three billion board feet of timber in Oregon and Washington alone, and a loss of 8,000 direct and 15,000 indirect jobs. Further, the Western Forest Industries Association, which represented industries that depended on public timber for survival, estimated that the spotted owl issue could result in 350 billion board feet of timber being held off the market. That timber had a value of $172 billion—about $95 million per pair of owls!

The WSLFTF delegates approved a resolution opposing listing the spotted owl as endangered and called for an evidentiary hearing on the mater. California was exempted from the owl decision because owls were found in secondary growth, rather than the old growth which environmentalists were seeking to lock up. An evidentiary hearing could reveal whether spotted owls could do well in Oregon and Washington's second and third growth stands, as they did in California.

In June, however, the U.S. Fish and Wildlife Service declared that the northern spotted owl was, indeed, a threatened species. They announced that they would hold up a specific plan for protection until July 23 because of concerns over the economic impact. In July, a federal task force traveled to Oregon, Washington, and California to listen to input from elected officials, timber industry representatives, and environmentalists. I was one of three representatives from Linn County invited to meet with the panel. I told the panel that government actions significantly reducing timber sale offerings would have catastrophic consequences to citizens in my district, in Oregon, and in the entire Pacific Northwest. I pointed out that 42% of the manufacturing jobs in my district were in wood products. Over 6,500 families in my district depended directly on wood products for their living and many more were indirectly affected by the health of the industry.

I presented the panel with letters from two voters in my district. One was from a 60-year-old logger, worried about being rehired if he lost his job. The other was from a 70-year-old man who feared for the jobs of his five grown children, four of whom worked in wood products. I also presented a recommendation from a Linn-Benton extension forester who urged that the 300 million board feet of timber that had been blown down in a recent storm should be considered in any forest management plan, as use of this "blown down" timber would mean jobs saved and a reduction in hazards from fire and insects.

A millworker from Dallas, Oregon told the panel that the state would face a bleak future if the government locked away too much old growth timber from logging in order to preserve spotted owl habitat. "You take timber away, you're cutting both legs out from under the state," he said. The President of Communities for a Great Oregon, who owned an equipment company in Sweet Home, told the federal panel that the rest of the country needed to know that Oregon had done a good job managing one of the nation's best renewable resources. He said, "We cannot discontinue harvesting timber. We have to convince America that we have been good stewards."

I wish I could tell you that common sense prevailed, but it didn't. Listing the owl as an endangered species eventually led to court orders stopping logging in national forests containing the Northern Spotted Owl. Eventually, these court orders would reduce harvests of timber in the Pacific Northwest by 90%, resulting in the loss of an estimated 30,000 jobs. The federal courts essentially took control of our forests, and the policy of "multiple use" of our federal timber lands gave way to a policy of no harvesting of the renewable resource of timber. The economy of rural Oregon and much of the Pacific Northwest continues to suffer to this day, and devastating wildfires have become much more common, because the forests have become overgrown. It is also worth noting that the U.S. Fish and Wildlife Service would eventually admit that the biggest threat came not from the timber industry, but from another owl—the barred owl—that preyed on the smaller spotted owl. Despite this admission, they would continue to insist that more land in our national forests be dedicated to protecting the spotted owl.

One of the state agencies that I frequently contacted on behalf of my constituents was the Oregon Department of Environmental Quality, a bureaucracy that seemed to specialize in outrageously restrictive regulations. One such excessive regulation came to my attention after DEQ officials determined that pulp mills using chlorine to bleach and strengthen pulp were discharging traces of dioxin, a chemical considered by some scientists as a possible carcinogen. In January, 1990, DEQ proposed limiting dioxin concentration downstream from pulp mills—including the Pope and Talbot mill in the community of Halsey in my district—to .013 parts dioxin to quadrillion parts water (the same proportion as one second in two billion years). This was despite the fact that the technology at the time could only detect dioxin levels greater than 10 parts per quadrillion—about 1000 times greater than the DEQ standard. The DEQ also proposed a $10,000 daily fine in case of a violation in the next two years.

Setting such a technically unattainable and unenforceable standard that was not backed up with scientific research made no sense, and it also threatened the economic health of my legislative district, as Pope and Talbot employed 700 people, and was also proposing a $400 million expansion of their Halsey plant. As a member on the Legislative Emergency Board I was able to request and secure funding for a study that would gather scientific data to determine the amount of toxic pollutants in the Willamette River, their sources, and whether they were at levels that were harmful to humans. The study, which was to be the most comprehensive of the river in nearly half a century, was conducted by an eleven member technical committee, chaired by former Multnomah County Judge John Beatty. Other members of the committee included representatives from cities, industry, agriculture, water resources, public health, fish and wildlife agencies, and environmental groups. The committee was charged with using the best scientific technology to gather data that would help in setting state policies that would balance the protection of the environment and public health with economic needs.

With the initiation of the study, the DEQ and Pope and Talbot were able to agree on a modified operating permit which limited dioxin and other emissions from the Halsey mill to .3 mg per day. (A common size aspirin tablet is 250mg!) This limit would mandate the company to cut their current maximum emission of dioxin by more than 50%. Pope and Talbot officials agreed this was a realistic limit, but were surprised when DEQ officials later tried to go back on the agreement and impose further restrictions. I brought both parties together in my office and spurred them to work out an agreement. Key to their eventual agreement was the knowledge that the Willamette River study would, upon its completion, provide a thorough scientific analysis of exactly what were the pollutants in the river, their levels, sources and impact, and the river's capacity to handle growth and economic needs.

I believe that the agreement between the DEQ and Pope and Talbot was a good example that we do not have to compromise environmental standards to have employment, as the mill permit adhered to the toughest standards in the world, yet allowed the company to maintain employment of 700 workers, begin a $50 million project to retrofit the plant to further reduce toxic chemicals, and opened the door for a possible $400 million expansion of the mill. I was delighted when mill officials publicly stated that without my "continuing gentle pressure, the process (of reaching an agreement) would have taken much longer, if it were accomplished at all."

Preliminary results of the Willamette River Study, which was conducted by Oregon State University, revealed measurable dioxin contamination had been found in some fish throughout the Willamette River system. The amount of dioxin accumulation were above levels outlined by the United States Environmental Protection Agency, but they were 25 times lower than levels specified by the US Food and Drug Administration for restricting fisheries, who, along with state health agency, were charged with issuing advisory rules on river contamination. These confusing and contradictory regulations showed federal agencies making excessive demands on industries without thorough scientific studies or co-ordination with each other, causing huge costs to businesses and threatening productivity, well paying jobs, capital investments and expansions.

Further, the study revealed that dioxin contamination levels found in the Willamette River system fish were up to 50 times lower than that of other river systems, including one in Texas that have pulp and paper manufacturing plants located on their shorelines. Researchers were also surprised to find similar dioxin levels at most of the six test points along the river. The dioxin concentration did not rise near the Pope and Talbot pulp plant in Halsey, about 22 miles south of Albany. The consistent 1 part per trillion concentration up and down river from Halsey showed that the pulp mill was not a "hot spot" or major point source for dioxin, and that the river was able to take care of the dioxin in it. Along with the manufacture of pulp and paper, sources of dioxin included wood preservatives, herbicides, and municipal incineration of plastics.

As I look back on my legislative years, I regard the Willamette River Study, initiated at my request in 1990, as one of my highest achievements, as its findings were essential to the safe use and protection of the river, which is Oregon's largest, flowing by more than 70% of the state's population. I am particularly proud of my successful efforts to provide funding for the Willamette River study in the 1991 through 1995 legislative session. The bi-annual $1.2 million funding was shared equally by the state, private industries, and municipal governments, and was matched by the federal government. During the 1995 legislative session I was able to convince my colleagues to continue funding the study after monies to do so had initially been removed from the DEQ budget.

The restored funding paid for continuing research, particularly on non-point source pollution, which entered the river not from any specific pipeline, but as runoff from fields, streets, parking lots, and the general countryside. Public meetings regarding the results and recommendations of the study of the Willamette River were held in Corvallis, Newberg, and Eugene after the 1995 session concluded. I stated that as population along the river increases over the next century, about one million more people are expected by 2050, we need to be vigilant in protecting the Willamette. Water quality is much improved from earlier in the century, when parts of the river were so polluted that they supported no life. The study was intended to develop models for determining how particular changes, such as added industries, would affect water quality in the river system. It also developed a baseline of information about river pollution. The study found that the water quality was fairly good in the upper and middle sections of the river, but poor in the lower stretches, including the Newberg Pool above the falls.

The steering committee recommended that the models be used as soon as possible, that the study be repeated every five years to detect changes in river quality, and that the health effects of river pollution on wildlife and humans be studied. Research from the Willamette River study also led Governor Kitzhaber in 1996 to form a Willamette River Task Force, which was charged with formulating policy recommendations on how to maintain the health of the river as the valley's population and number of industries grew. I was certain that the Governor's Task Force would benefit from the findings, models, and scientific data collected by the Willamette River Study as they formulated sound policy recommendations. In fact the study subsequently led to the creation of the Willamette Restoration Initiative (WRI), which was empowered by Governor Kitzhaber to take actions when several species of salmon, steelhead, and other fish were listed as threatened or endangered.

One of my goals for my final session in the Oregon State Legislature in 2001 was to take additional steps to ensure the safe use and protection of the health of the Willamette River. There were a number of worthwhile wide-ranging research and study projects that were deserving of sate funding, but the state's economy was not strong, and resources were limited. In light of that reality, I decided to focus on much needed research, and authored legislation that provided funding to conduct a study on fish deformity in the Willamette River. Fish deformities in certain portions of the Willamette had gone unresolved for nearly half a century. I believed it was critical to find the cause or causes of these deformities so that we could assess options for the protection of the fish and to determine whether the deformities indicated a threat to public health.

My legislative colleagues agreed with my concerns, and both the House and Senate overwhelmingly passed the legislation mandating the study. It takes the Governor's signature to transform a bill into law, and I was surprised when Governor Kitzhaber vetoed the bill. The Governor stated that he believed that the Oregon Water Enhancement Board (OWEB) rather than the legislature should determine which projects affecting Oregon rivers deserved funding, and OWEB had listed the fish deformity study as 11th of 12 priorities.

I disagreed with the OWEB ranking and with the Governor's veto, as I believed that preserving Oregon's unique quality of life meant ensuring we had clean water: water that is drinkable, fishable, and swimmable. With a never-say-die attitude and using the knowledge gained during my years on the Ways and Means Committee, I attached a budget note to the OWEB appropriation package directing them to provide the $500,000 in funding to the three-year Willamette River fish deformity research and to report back to the legislature on the development and progress of the research. The funding was available due to interest earnings from bonds for parks improvement designated for research.

The mystery of what was causing deformed fish would be solved in January 2004 when scientists at Oregon State University would complete the study and report that the fish were deformed not because of pesticides or other pollutants—but because of parasites that infested their bones. A few weeks later, the *Albany Democrat Herald* would run the following editorial:

"Researchers at Oregon State University have done everybody a huge favor by finding the source of fish deformities in the Willamette River. Their conclusion that the abnormalities in some juvenile fish are caused by two kinds of parasites, not by pollutants such as pesticides is a milestone. It keeps efforts to clean up the river from going off in a wrong and useless direction. Let us remember who is responsible for the effort to get to the bottom of this question, which has cropped up in one Willamette River study after another for years. Bone deformities that resembled those caused by the parasite were identified in museum specimens from the 1850's. The driving force was Mae Yih, the state senator from Albany who drove her critics mad by her persistence, and who never had trouble getting re-elected because voters knew that once Mae said something she would stick with it, no matter what....It was Mae Yih who got the Legislature to pass a bill requiring the study of fish deformities in 2001. And when Governor John Kitzhaber vetoed the bill, she persisted by requesting the research through a budget note in the Water Enhancement Board's budget."

I was also heartened to receive a letter from Oregonians for Food and Shelter who wrote that the "results of the study will now shatter the ongoing rhetoric by environmental activists who claimed the deformities were caused by pesticides and dioxins. Many environmental groups who were so quick to point fingers at farmers, foresters and industry can now eat their words."

Throughout my years in the legislature I was very proud to be considered a "friend of the farmer" and to consistently receive top ratings from the Oregon Farm Bureau. Oregon's Willamette Valley is one of best agricultural areas in the country and was key to a strong economy—a fact that legislators and state officials who came from urban Portland often forgot. During the 1993 session, I was dismayed to discover that Governor Roberts' proposed budget severely reduced funding of the Soil and Water Conservation and totally eliminated funding of the Animal Damage Control programs. As you know, I was almost always a proponent of reducing bureaucratic budgets, but these two programs were two of the best managed in the state, and they were of vital importance to Oregon farmers. Studies showed that farmers lost some 3,200 sheep, 9,900 lambs, and 4,500 calves to coyotes and other predators each year. These numbers would have skyrocketed without an Animal Damage Control Program. I worked with other Ways and Means Committee members who represented rural districts to find $200,000 to restore the Soil and Water Conservation Program and $300,000 to preserve the Animal Damage Control Program.

One of the responsibilities of the State Senate is the power to approve or disapprove certain Gubernatorial appointments. While I usually believed in giving governors leeway in appointing members to statewide boards and commissions, I did believe that the members of boards and commissions that oversaw agriculture and natural resource issues should have experience and in-depth knowledge in the issues that they were overseeing. In 1994, when the Senate was divided between 16 Democrats and 14 Republicans, I joined with Republican Senators in blocking several of Governor Roberts appointments to the Oregon State Board of Forestry, the Oregon Water Resources Commission, and the Land Conservation and Development Commission because we believed they didn't have the necessary experience or background. Many constituents had urged me to take such action, and with the natural resource industry facing such challenging times, I said it was a poor time to take a chance on management of our forestlands and our water supply.

Priority #5: Connecting Oregon and China

The history of trade and a friendly and cultural relationship between my birth country and my adopted country is a long and complicated one. Trade between the United States and China began soon after American independence, with tea, silk, porcelain ware being the most important Chinese commodities. American missionaries played a large role in establishing friendly and cultural relationships between the two countries. As America became industrialized in the mid-to-late 19th century, large numbers of Chinese immigrated to the United States to work as laborers in industries such as railroads and gold mines. Many Americans soon began to resent the competition of the Chinese workers, who were extremely industrious and were willing to accept low wages, and in 1882, the United States Congress passed into law the Chinese Exclusion Act, which strictly limited the number of Chinese immigrants coming into America and prevented immigrants already in America from becoming citizens. It was not until World War II, when China became an American ally in the war against Japan, that the Chinese Exclusion Act was repealed in 1943. When the Communists took control of China following World War II, relations between the two countries deteriorated again, and the governments would not communicate until President Nixon opened the door to diplomacy with his historic 1972 trip to China.

In the forty-four years since President Nixon's visit, the relationship between the United States and China has experienced both strong and weak moments, but the diplomatic and economic ties have continued to grow. I take pride in the fact that my twenty-six years in the Oregon legislature allowed me to do everything I could to forge richer relations between my beloved adopted country and my mother country.

I began this mission because of the pride I felt in my Chinese heritage, but I continued it because I understood first hand the atrocity and devastation of war, corruption, and rampant inflation under a dictatorship where few lived in wealth and the vast majority lived in extreme poverty. I knew the importance of friendly relations, cultural understanding, trust and free trade among nations that would bring peace, harmony and prosperity in the world. I also knew that stronger relations between Oregon and China made a great deal of economic sense. Ideally located in the Pacific Rim, Oregon's geographic proximity and our agricultural, forestry, and high technology industries, as well as our environmental protection services, would be mutually beneficial as China opened its doors to American and western businesses.

As you will read in the forthcoming pages, forging better relations between Oregon and China was a lengthy decades-long process that involved much hard work, and constantly battling some legislators and state bureaucrats who were locked into an outdated belief that China was an adversary, rather than a tremendous friendly export market of Oregon and the United States. Despite some early setbacks, I persisted and am very proud to report that according to the International Trade Administration, 2015 annual exports from Oregon businesses to China were $4.8 billion. While I certainly cannot take credit for all of those exports, I know that my efforts made a positive difference in changing attitudes, and in opening doors. When you are through reading this section, I hope you will be very proud of what your grandmother accomplished.

My legislative efforts began in 1979 when I was invited to attend a luncheon reception, accompanied by your grandfather Stephen, in Seattle, Washington for Deng Xiao Ping, then the Vice Premier of China, during the final stop of his first visit to the United States. Before leaving for Seattle, I obtained the signatures of 57 of the 60 members of the Oregon House of Representatives, including Speaker of the House Hardy Myers, on a resolution welcoming the Vice Premier to the United States, and inviting him to visit the beautiful green state of Oregon in the near future. Because of very tight security at the luncheon, I did not have the opportunity to personally present the legislative welcome resolution, but I made sure that it was delivered to him by U.S. State Department officials.

At the end of the 1979 session, an incident that was initially embarrassing to me actually resulted in me being placed in a position that better enabled me to improve the ties between China and Oregon. In the final hours of the session, the Speaker of the House announced his list of members who would serve until the 1981 session on the "Joint Legislative Emergency Board," which was empowered to make important budgetary decisions during the interim. The Speaker had promised me this appointment at the beginning of the session in return for my commitment to vote for him as Speaker. As it turned out, he made a similar promise to one other member, and the House eventually voted down my selection. This shabby treatment led me briefly think about resigning, but then I remembered the words of my friend who was a county commissioner that in politics you win some, and you lose some, and if you remained persistent, you would win in the end. The very next day, the Speaker called and offered me the Co-Chair position of the Joint Legislative Trade and Economic Development Committee for the interim. I had a great interest in the work of that committee, as I saw it as an avenue to promote friendly relations and trade between Oregon and China, and I immediately accepted.

A couple of months later, I learned that a delegation led by Ron Yi Ren, the Chairman of the China International Trust and Investment Corporation, would be visiting five large cities in the United States, including San Francisco. I knew that a top advisor to the corporation and one of Ron's sisters had both attended the same high school in Shanghai as I did. I sent a message to Ron's top advisor, promoting Oregon's forestry and agriculture industries and inviting his delegation to visit Salem following their visit to San Francisco. I was delighted that he accepted my offer.

As Co-Chair of the Joint Legislative Trade and Economic Development Committee, I hosted the welcoming reception for the delegation in the Governor's ceremonial office. Governor Atiyeh, who had recently returned from a trade mission to Asia that did not include a visit to China, and who had previously remarked that China's potential as a market was "overrated," was very gracious. Chairman Ron was equally gracious, stressing that the Governor's remarks were in the past. All in all, it was a very memorable day, and one that set the stage for more trade missions.

In November 1981, I traveled to China with a delegation organized by the United States Wheat Growers Association with the hope of opening up markets for Oregon and Northwest wheat. Oregon annually produced about 70 million bushels of wheat, with about 85% of that crop being exported. Oregon wheat had a high protein content (11.5% compared to 1% protein content in rice) that made it a natural for the Chinese market. However, the Chinese government had refused to purchase large quantities of Northwest wheat, based on their belief that our "wheat was infected with a minor crop disease called TCK smut."

From Steve's many years of experience in dealing with Chinese businessmen and leaders, I knew that the way to convince them of the good quality of our wheat was not through high-pressure sales, but through data backed up by science and research. Therefore, I invited Dr. Edward Trione, a research wheat scientist from Oregon State University, to join me on the trip, and I paid all his expenses. While we were in China, we met with top agriculture officials and presented his research as to why TKC Smut did not pose a danger to China's wheat crop. For TCK Smut disease to develop, it takes special climatic conditions, such as a 60 to 90-day snow cover period, which China rarely has, and temperatures around 0-5 degrees. Large quantities of wheat that were contaminated with TCK spores was shipped to China from 1930-1950, but there is no indication of TCK smut in China. This trip was taken in conjunction with the U. S. Wheat League's sponsorship of two Chinese scientists to visit Oregon State University and participate in research and field studies for two years.

In December 1981, Hu Ding Yi, the Consul General of the People's Republic of China (PRC), who was stationed in San Francisco, visited Oregon with his wife, and accepted my invitation to speak to the Albany Chamber of Commerce at 6:45 in the morning, and to spend the night before his speech at our home. Grandpa cooked his famous gourmet Chinese noodles for breakfast for them.

In 1983, we sponsored a full scholarship for a Chinese forestry student to come to the OSU Forestry Department for a year's study upon the recommendation of the Forestry Department Chairman, after his return from his visit to China. There is a dire need for reforestation in China for timber and erosion control.

The more time I spent devoting myself to building and improving better understanding and friendly trade relations between Oregon and China, the more opportunities were presented to me to do more. Also, my 1982 election to a four-year term in the Oregon State Senate, meant that I did not have to dedicate myself to campaigning in 1984. As a result, I was able to spend a great deal of time that year forging a stronger partnership between Oregon and China.

The year kicked off in exciting fashion when, in January, upon the invitation of the U.S. China People's Friendship Association, I flew to Washington, D.C. at my own expense to attend the official welcoming ceremony for Zhao Xi Yang, Premier of the People's Republic of China. The Association invited the two Oregon United States Senators, but they were unable to attend. I was then invited, and was delighted to accept. As I arrived, I spotted Hu Ding Yi, who, as PRC Consul General, visited Oregon, stayed at our home, and spoke to the Albany Chamber of Commerce in 1981. He was now a high-ranking official in the PRC Embassy, and he invited me to sit in the section reserved for dignitaries. Following the welcoming ceremony, I joined others in that section in being ushered inside the White House to meet the Premier in a smaller and more intimate reception.

Needless to say, it was an unforgettable day. I will always remember the extravagant array of food, the beautiful ice sculptures in the form of dragons and eagles, and how exciting it was to go through the receiving line and to be able to greet President Reagan, Mrs. Reagan, and the Premier. I was able to speak to the Premier in Mandarin, and told him that I was born in Shanghai, served as an Oregon State Senator, and invited him to visit Oregon. He responded with a big smile. I couldn't help but think how proud my father and mother would have been to see their daughter at the White House. Later in the day, I attended another reception at the Chinese Embassy in Washington, D.C., and a lavish evening reception the Premier hosted for President Reagan in the ballroom of the Vista International Hotel. At these receptions and others that were held during the Premier's visit, I was able to meet with several high ranking officials of the Chinese government, to converse with them in their native dialect. I spoke Cantonese to the PRC Ambassador, and in Shanghainese to the foreign minister. (I learned and spoke three Chinese dialects when I was growing up; Cantonese with my mother, since she was a native of Hongkong; Shanghainese with my dad and others in Shanghai; and Mandarin, which I learned in school.) I also presented the Ambassador with a book about Oregon, an introductory letter about the world renowned mid-Willamette Valley grass seed industry, and I invited them to visit the beautiful green state of Oregon. I also introduced myself to Vice President George H.W. Bush, who had previously served as U.S. Ambassador to China, and he gave me the longest handshake of my life. It must have lasted more than two minutes!

The very next month, Tang Shu Bei, the San Francisco-based Consul General of the People's Republic of China, visited Oregon for four days—two of them were spent in my legislative district. His office had asked me to arrange his itinerary, and I put together a busy schedule of visits and meetings devoted to paper and wood products manufacturing, forestry management, and grass seed production. One day was high-lighted by a potluck lamb barbecue hosted by 35 grass seed farm families at a Tangent grade school gymnasium.

Oregon is the nation's leading producer of grass seeds, annually producing between 275 and 300 million pounds that are high in purity and germination rate. The Consul General believed that the mid-valley grass seed might be a key to expanding trade relations between China and the United States and to improve the standard of living of its huge population. His belief was based in the knowledge that in order to produce more meat and dairy products, China needed to reclaim much of its barren soil, par-ticularly in the northwestern region where work needed to be done in developing and improving its pasture land, and containing the expansion of the large desert area.

Consul General Tong also said that China was most interested in trading with Ore-gon in lumber and forest products. With a population five times that of the United States, there was a great demand for lumber in China to build homes, bridges and rail-roads. Only 13% of China is forested due to the continuous cutting of forests that had occurred over the past one hundred years of war China had experienced during the Ching dynasty, the nationalist revolution, the Japanese invasion, WWII, and the com-munist revolution. In comparison, 43% of land in the United States is forested. In need of strong reforestation efforts, China was extremely interested in improving genetics of trees and technology for reforestation and forest management.

The success of his visit and my continued work in promoting trade and friendly relations led Consul General Tang Shubei to ask me to arrange technical exchange visits by five local foresters and the same number of grass seed growers to China in the fall of 1984 and the spring of 1985. The Chinese government hosted their two-week long visits to inner Mongolia and other cold and arid areas in the northwestern provinces. I then worked with Consul General Tang in arranging a return visit that same year by Chinese foresters and grass seed growers to Oregon.

One of my legislative victories in the 1983 session was the passage of legislation creating a "sister state" relationship between Oregon and Fujian province of the Peo-ple's Republic of China. The Fujian province, with about 26 million people, had ten times the population of Oregon with only half the land area. It would be a huge market for Oregon's agricultural products, as 80% of the area of the province was too mountainous to produce crops, and more suitable for development of pastureland. I urged Oregon Governor Vic Atiyeh to travel to China to personally sign the sister state relationship agreement and he consented to do so as part of a trade mission to Japan and China in September 1984. I accompanied the Governor for much of the trip, and was very pleased with the connections that were made in China. In Beijing, we met with Premier Zhao and our friend Ron Yi Ren, Chairman of the China International Trust and Investment Corporation, who visited Oregon in 1979. One of the banquets for the governor was hosted by Jiang Zi Ming, then minister of the electronic industry, who would become President of the People's Republic of China from 1993 to 2003. Out of the nine-course banquet, my favorite dish was large prawns served in a "bird's nest," which was made up of thinly shredded woven fried potatoes. It was delicious and beautiful to look at. I brought my photo with Premier Zhao, which had been taken at the White House reception hosted by President and Mrs. Reagan earlier in January, and asked him to autograph the picture for me. He graciously agreed.

Everywhere I visited in China I gave out samples of Oregon grass seeds and super fast growth tree seeds packaged by Oregon companies (with the business cards of the companies attached). The samples were well received. However, quite often grass seeds leaked into my wardrobe and seeped out of creases in my clothes, giving out hints that I represented the grass seed industry in my senate district. Whenever I gave the superfast growth tree seed samples I was advised to say, "When you plant these seeds, jump back! They grow super fast!"

Two months after our visit, Governor Hu Ping of the Fujian province, accompanied by a 17-member delegation, would make a reciprocal visit to Oregon. I was again able to arrange a day of meetings in my district, and further cemented ties between China and the mid-Willamette Valley. The local grade schools arranged to have students welcome Governor Hu Ping in Chinese, waving small flags of China and America at a grass seed company in Tangent and also greeted him at the luncheon where he spoke to the Albany Chamber of Commerce. Here, the schoolchildren presented him and the members of his delegation with bouquets of red roses. The children's welcome was a real hit. Governor Hu Ping and his delegation were very surprised and pleased. A photo of Governor Hu Ping being greeted by the schoolchildren was printed in the local newspaper and presented to him. The Governor autographed it with the Chinese words, "Dear little friends, study hard and move upwards every day."

Another valuable connection occurred in 1988, when a Harrisburg grass seed grower who had earlier traveled to China as part of an exchange trip, donated 350 pounds of tall fescue seeds to be planted on the front lawn of the American Embassy in Beijing. Betty Bao Lord, who was the wife of Winston Lord, then the United States

Ambassador to China, wrote me in May 1988 to let me know the lawn had been reju-
venated with Oregon grass seeds, and she hoped it would be fully established in time
for the annual July 4 celebration at the American embassy, so she and the Ambassador
would be "standing proud by the beautiful green lawn." A small sign would also be
posted stating that the lawn was established by Oregon grass seeds and the name of the
Oregon grower's company.

I had met Mrs. Lord in Beijing the past August, during a Women to Women
Exchange Program led by Madame Anna Chenault of Washington, D.C. When Mrs.
Lord hosted us for lunch, I took the opportunity to give her a sample packet of Oregon
grass seeds, as I always did wherever I went. She made the request of grass seed for
the Embassy's lawn at that time. She provided data regarding lawn size, water avail-
ability during dry months, annual rainfall and temperature in Beijing, type of mower
used and related factors to the Oregon grower who sent the variety that had good
drought tolerance and was easy to maintain.

This project was another step in my campaign to encourage trade between Oregon
and China, as if the lawn flourished, it could prompt a positive response from others in
China who were interested in such a lawn. I am very proud to report that the Oregon
Seed Council reported that my constant efforts to promote Willamette Valley grass
seed made a positive difference, as Oregon grass seed exports to China increased by
a remarkable 4,467% in just four short years between 1993 and 1997.

One of my most memorable journeys to China occurred in 1992, when I organized
a 14-day legislative friendship and trade delegation visit led by then Senate President
John Kitzhaber and House Speaker Larry Campbell. We were traveling at the invitation
of the government of the Fujian Province, who hosted the delegation four out of the six
cities we visited. Individual members of the delegation covered their international travel
expenses, and no state funds were used for the trip. Our itinerary included Fuzhou, the
capital of Fujian Province, as well as the cities of Quanzhou and Xiamen. In addition,
the delegation visited Shanghai, one of China's largest and most important commercial
centers; Xian, where the first Emperor's tomb and his 6,000 terra cotta soldiers were
buried; and Beijing, the national capital.

The main purpose of this visit and others I organized with the help of the Director
of the Fujian Province Foreign Affairs Office was to reinforce the message that China's
huge population and booming economy offered growing opportunities for profitable
trade. This message was abundantly clear in Fujian Province, which had a population
of over 26 million, and contained several "special economic zones" in which foreign
trade and investment were given privileges in tax reductions and fewer regulations. In
one such area, near the port city of Xiamen, the special economic zone had attracted
more than $2.2 billion in foreign investment and created tens of thousands of new jobs.
The delegation saw a new city of hundreds of factories, offices and apartments, sym-

bolizing more than 1,000 projects. This was a city where just ten years ago there was only farmland. Interestingly, Jia Qinlin, who was Governor of the Fujian Province and our host during our visit in 1992 had risen through the ranks and is now the mayor of Beijing, and the fourth highest leader in China.

The value of connections made during trips such as this one can be seen in the fact that during the 1992 visit to China, I became reacquainted with Professor Peter Hue of Beijing Agriculture University. Professor Hue had become a friend of mine when he studied at the Oregon State University School of Agriculture, and he asked me to help Liu Zi Xue, a high ranking official in the Ministry of Agriculture's Grassland Division in his request to come to OSU to study about grass seed production and testing. When I returned to Oregon, I arranged for several grass seed companies to sponsor the official on a six-month study. Liu later became President of Beijing Clover Seed and Turf Company, where he bought grass seed supplies for farms, municipalities, parks and recreation districts, and government agencies. He told me whenever we visited him in Beijing he always looked favorably on Oregon farms and businesses. He bought 10,000 tons of grass seed from Oregon in 1999 alone. Professor Peter Hue also pioneered in setting up pilot plots for a variety of Oregon grass seeds at Beijing Agriculture University in consultation with faculty members of Oregon State University. More connections were made several months later when eleven officials from Fujian Province traveled to Oregon for a five-day visit to explore trade opportunities.

Along with sending agriculture products to China, I was also pleased to be involved in a program that sent books. In October of 1993, the Oregon State Library Foundation shipped 17,000 books to Fujian Province, our sister state. By coincidence, when a ceremony was held marking the official send-off of the books, I was hosting a 10-member Fujian economic and trade exchange delegation on their visit to Oregon. I escorted the delegation to the ceremony, and Chen Guangyi, chairman of the Standing Committee of Fujian Province of People's Congress said, "This will deepen our understanding and friendship, and we can learn a lot from these books." That evening, I also joined with the Oregon Seed Council and Oregon Women for Agriculture in hosting a barbecue dinner for the delegation at the Tangent Elementary School gymnasium.

One of my most memorable visits to China occurred in late 1994 when I traveled to Fujian province. During a busy schedule of meetings where I promoted the opening of new markets for Oregon's grass seed farmers, forest product companies and food processors, I was honored to be one of the first two individuals named an "Honorary Citizen of Fujian Province." That same year, Jia Qinglin, the Governor of Fujian Province, traveled to Oregon, where he met Governor Kitzhaber and offered to provide office space and local staff in the provincial capital of Fuzhou, if Oregon would provide a trade representative to work there. I believed the opening of such an office would be of great benefit to Oregon companies and farmers looking to do business in China, and in the 1995 legislative session I succeeded in obtaining funding to staff the jointly operated office.

My effort to forge and strengthen trade relations between Oregon and China was sometimes a lonely one. A number of the bureaucrats in the Oregon Economic Development Department were very focused on trade relations with Japan, and they gave little attention to China. Given the ever-increasing growth of China's economy and the fact that the population of China was ten times that of Japan, I believed they were very shortsighted. Our neighboring states Washington and California were leading the nation in trade with China, while Oregon's total exports to China ranked only 22nd in the nation.

Despite the shortsighted bureaucrats in the Oregon Economic Development Department, I continued to advocate for closer ties between Oregon and China, and was delighted when a series of events made 1997 a very eventful and productive year.

One of the most unforgettable experiences of my life was the journey that Steve and I made in the summer of 1997 to observe the ceremonies marking the end of the British colonial rule of Hong Kong, and the reunification of Hong Kong to Chinese sovereignty. For me, this was a very emotional ceremony, as I had visited my grandparents in Hong Kong many times in my childhood. I recall that on one visit, my grandfather had pointed out a humiliating sign in Queen Victoria Park that read "No dogs or Chinese allowed." When the British flag was lowered and the Chinese flag went up and the national anthem began to play, I jumped up and down with joy and tears were rolling down my cheeks. While at the ceremonies, I participated in the U.S. Consul General's reception, where then Secretary of State Madeline Albright spoke and expressed the friendship of the United States and support for democracy in Hong Kong.

I attended the Hong Kong handover ceremony as a member of the Committee of 100, a New York City based organization, which consists of prominent Chinese-Americans who are successful in business, politics, academics and the arts. About 15 members of the committee were in Hong Kong for the ceremonies. Your grandfather and I also attended an unforgettable concert by the Asian Youth Orchestra, who played a special symphony written by the renowned composer and conductor Tan Dann. As part of the concert, sixty-four pieces of 2400-year-old Zeng Dynasty bronze bells were used and paired with 100 children's voices. The bronze bells were played to symbolize the past and the children's voices symbolized the future. I predicted at the time that Hong Kong's prominence as an economic powerhouse would only continue to grow—and the events of the past 18 years have proven my prediction correct.

On July 14, 1997—just ten days after I returned from Hong Kong—Fujian province Vice Governor Wang Jian Shuang and a seven member high level provincial delegation arrived in Oregon for a four day visit. I attended a series of meetings and banquets that were hosted and attended by Governor Kitzhaber, and interested business firms.

Then, in October 1997, I was joined by seven of my legislative colleagues and their spouses on an Oregon Legislative Trade and Friendship Delegation visit to China. The delegation included the top two legislative leaders—Senate President Brady Adams and House Speaker Lynn Lundquist. The two-week long trip came about because of the visit I made to the Fujian province in December 1994, when I was awarded an honorary citizenship. During that trip, the Director of Foreign Affairs invited me to return with a delegation of eight legislators, spouses, and small business owners from our districts, and promised that the Fujian government would host the legislators' stay in Fujian and arrange for VIP discount and treatment in Shanghai, Xian and Beijing. When I told President Adams about that offer, he expressed interest and gave me the go ahead to plan the trip. Making the countless arrangements that were necessary to ensure the success of the trip was almost a full-time job for several months!

Just arranging four official visits in one afternoon on a national holiday weekend in Beijing involved contacting eight agencies in the United States and China. In addition, there was a 16-hour time difference between the Fujian Province and Oregon, so many phone calls had to be made around midnight in Oregon in order to reach the Fujian officials during office hours. On top of all the details that needed to be taken care of, the Director of Sister-State Relationships in the Fujian Province did not speak English! I had to translate his memos—including proposed itinerary and cost estimates—into English so the legislators and business delegation members making the trip could understand them. To make it worse, the director often ignored my repeated requests for appointments in Beijing. It was not until two weeks before our departure when the Fujian government finally re-assigned an English speaking coordinator to work with me.

Our itinerary included visits to several cities in the Fujian province, including the provincial capital of Fuzhou, and the special economic zone of Xiamen, as well as stops in Shanghai, Xian, and Beijing. While in Beijing, we met with Mayor Jia Qin Ling, who was one of the top leaders in China, and who had visited Oregon in 1994 when he was serving as Governor of the Fujian province. An elegant cocktail reception and buffet dinner in Beijing for Chinese and American international trade business leaders and government officials was hosted by Nike. We also found time to visit the Great Wall, the Ming Tomb, ride a two-hump camel, and buy "three snake" wine in a famous resort in the Fujian Province. As the name indicates, there are three snakes in the bottle of wine, which are meant to provide extra nutrition for eye health! Speaker Lynn Lundquist and I shared in the purchase of the "three snake wine" and agreed to drink it when there was an occasion for celebration in Oregon. Lynn kept the bottle and I am sorry to report that we never did get around to drinking it before he passed away in 2013.

Throughout the trip, I was constantly working to make sure that everything was as close to perfection as possible. All the hours and planning I put in to organizing the trip paid off when Senator Adams, who was diabetic, left his insulin bag on a tour bus in Shanghai. As usual, I had written down the name and office and home phone numbers of our tour guide, and was able to call him at his home at night to tell him of the problem. He, in turn, called the bus driver, who found the bag, and brought it to our hotel by taxi at midnight! Needless to say, Senator Adams was extremely relieved to have his much needed insulin back.

Perhaps the most lasting memory of the trip was a ten-course Peking duck banquet hosted by Liu Zi Xue, the general manager and president of Beijing Clover Seed and Turf Company. As mentioned earlier, I had helped arrange the sponsorship that allowed him to attend a six-month study program at Oregon State University. Along with expressing his thanks by hosting the banquet, he also annually purchased large amounts of grass seed from Oregon. The main course of the banquet was a roast duck, and in accordance with the Chinese tradition, the most honored guest had the privilege of eating the duck's brain. As the leaders of the delegation, House Speaker Lundquist and Senate President Adams both were good sports and accepted the honor of eating half the brain each!

At the conclusion of the trip, all members of the legislative delegation—Democrats and Republicans alike—agreed that the visit had been a great success. The benefits included strengthening the market for Oregon products like wheat, grass seed, vegetable seed, timber and hardwood flooring; discussing the possibility of direct airline flights from China to Portland; and forming ties that would encourage trade between small businesses. My legislative colleagues seemed to have a much better appreciation and understanding of the long and rich history and culture of China, their booming economy, and the friendliness and warmth of the people they met there.

Just a week after returning from China, I attended a luncheon in Los Angeles in honor of Chinese President Jiang Zi Ming. While I was not able to personally greet the president due to tight security rules, I did leave him a present of a small package of Oregon grass seeds with a letter explaining the superior purity and high germination qualities of those seeds, which made them ideal for use in the development of parks, golf courses, pasture lands, and in controlling erosion.

A very busy year of strengthening connections between Oregon and China concluded in December 1997 when I organized a reception in the State Capitol Building for a delegation led by Chinese Consul General Wang Yon Qui. Senate President Adams and House Speaker Lundquist were hosts of the reception where many state officials, legislators and businesses were invited to attend.

Another highlight occurred in April 1999 when I traveled to Washington, D.C. to participate in festivities welcoming Chinese Premier Zhu Rong Ji. I attended an outdoor White House South Lawn 19-gun salute welcome ceremony, a luncheon hosted by United States Secretary of State Madeline Albright, and a dinner hosted by The

Committee of 100. As I went through the receiving line, I was able to introduce myself to the Premier, who had formerly served as mayor of Shanghai, in both Shanghai and Mandarin dialect, as I presented him through his aides letters from Governor Kitzhaber and Senate President Brady Adams containing Oregon grass seed and superfast growth tree seeds. I joined with the director of the Oregon Economic Development Department in the signing of a memorandum of understanding with the Chinese Minister of Science and Technology establishing in Oregon a China-U.S. Center for Sustainable Development (CUCSD). The purpose of this center was to develop cooperative projects to advance environmental protection and sustainable development and practices in such areas as agriculture, forestry, environmental protection, energy, land use planning, transportation, and the marine environment.

Just a few weeks later, I traveled to New York City for a meeting of the Committee of 100. There, I was able to meet with World Bank President James Wolfensohn, who was one of the speakers on the Committee's program, and inform him about the CUCSD so that he could assist us in Oregon if he knew of any funding for projects in China in the area of air or water pollution reduction or infrastructure needs.

One of the most frustrating experiences during my legislative career was my long effort to establish an Oregon trade office in China. Each time I traveled to China, I saw that other states were being more aggressive and more successful than Oregon in encouraging and increasing trade relations. For example, the United States Department of Commerce had opened an international trade center in downtown Shanghai, and the states of Michigan, Maryland, and Washington were renting space in the center. I believed that having a permanent presence in Shanghai was a smart business move and renting space in the United States Department of Commerce International Trade Center would enhance up-to-date research information, build trust and credibility, and lead to more contacts and opportunities for trade and friendly relationships.

My efforts to open a trade office began in 1994, when Governor Jia Qinglin of Fujian province, our sister state, visited Oregon, and proposed the establishment of a joint trade office in the provincial capital of Fuzhou. During the 1995 legislative session, I requested and received funding of $65,000 to staff the joint office. After the session, however, the Governor and Department of Economic Development Department claimed that a "decline in revenue," forced them to revoke the funding.

I came back in the 1997 session with legislation that would establish and provide $170,000 in funding to start an Oregon trade office in Shanghai. The money was appropriated, but Governor Kitzhaber declined to open up the office, saying that he wanted the International Trade Commission to first establish criteria for opening and staffing trade offices in China. Governor Kitzhaber traveled to China in 1998, and when he returned he announced that he thought it would be premature and too "risky" to open a trade office there. In my view, the Governor didn't understand that with risk comes opportunity.

Finally, other legislators and businesses agreed with me, and during the 1999 session, emboldened by the positive recommendation of a China market study, which OEDD had commissioned at my request, I was successful in achieving passage of a bill which provide funding for the Oregon Economic Development Department to contract with a consultant to represent Oregon businesses doing business in China. It did not achieve all I wanted, as opening an Oregon state office in the United States Department of Commerce International Trade Center in downtown Shanghai would have carried much more prestige, credibility and been more effective. However, it was late in the session when the bill was discussed, and I reluctantly accepted the compromise legislation as a step forward. The bill required the contracted trade consultant to make a recommendation to Oregon Economic and Community Development Department and the Legislature by January 1, 2001, on whether a permanent Oregon trade office should be opened and, if so, the recommended timing, location, staffing, and budget needs.

When the 1999 session concluded in July, I immediately began work as a member of the 11-member task force, who had been appointed to select the trade consultant who would represent Oregon in China. Our requirements included that the consultant be well versed with American business practices; have extensive contacts with Chinese companies and government officials; be able to travel to America for orientation and follow-up visits; and be able to promote sales of Oregon's products and services in our four key industries of agriculture, forestry, high-tech and environmental protection services. We also specified that the priority of the consultant was to help small and medium-size companies since many large companies, such as Nike, Motorola, Freightliner, CH2M Hill, and many others already had offices in China. I also insisted that the consultant would need to prepare an outcome report that detailed the number of jobs created by the Oregon companies who were assisted by the consultant.

In November 1999, I traveled to Shanghai to join executives from the OECDD in interviewing and ranking the five finalists for the job of representative. After initial interviews of all five candidates, we invited the three top candidates to return the next day for a second interview. While there, we paid a courtesy call to Shanghai's vice-mayor and informed him that we would soon be selecting an Oregon-China trade consultant. We also discussed Oregon's signing of a memorandum of understanding in April with the Chinese Minister of Science and Technology establishing in Oregon a China-U.S. Center for Sustainable Development (CUCSD), which took place during Premier Zhu Rong Ji's visit to the U.S. and conference with vice president Al Gore regarding cooperation in environmental protection and sustainable economic development. A Sustainable Economic Development Seminar in Shanghai in May 2000, when an Oregon legislative trade delegation was scheduled to visit, was suggested, and the vice mayor was very enthusiastic and supportive of the idea.

Upon returning to Oregon, the panel met a final time and chose Jepsen and Company, a 104-year-old Hong Kong based trading company, which had nine offices in China and a strong track record of assisting small companies succeed in the China market. Jepsen and Company managers then traveled to Oregon in December to receive an overview of Oregon's economy, to meet with key governmental and business leaders, and to sponsor a workshop for businesses interested in entering the Chinese market. I made sure that their schedule included a trip to the Willamette Valley for a full understanding of our grass seed industry, companies and farms. Most importantly, we scheduled seminars and workshops on how to do business with China in Salem and Portland. I was delighted that over 130 highly motivated and interested businesses attended the seminars.

Along with the many business related trips I took to China, your grandfather and I also made several personal journeys to our mother country. One of the most memorable was in the fall of 1999 when we traveled to China with our good friends Roger and Sharon Reid. Roger was a highly respected attorney in Albany and a strong Democrat, and he managed every one of my campaigns for state representative and state senator. It was his advice to go door-to-door campaigning that led to my first election. Your grandfather mentioned to me that he thought it would be fun to take Roger and Sharon to China as a thank you for his hard work and wisdom. I immediately agreed and began planning the trip that would eventually take us to Hong Kong, Shanghai, Beijing, and Xian from September 27 to October 7. There is a Chinese saying that "in the autumn, the sky is high and the air is crisp," and that was the case during this enjoyable visit. As it turned out, the 50th anniversary of the founding of the People's Republic of China coincided with our trip. I was invited to the VIP platform to observe the 50th anniversary grand parade led by President Jiang Zi Ming and later that evening, from our hotel rooms near Tiananmen Square, we were able to view an amazing and overwhelming two-hour fireworks show where the fireworks were shot into the sky from six different locations in the city.

As my legislative career neared its end, I was pleased to make a special effort to ensure that trade between Oregon and China would continue to grow. In May 2000, at the request of Senate President Adams, I organized and arranged a follow-up visit to China by a 28 member delegation which included five legislators (among them the President of the Senate, the Senate Majority Leader, and the Senate Minority Leader),spouses, ten business leaders representing a variety of agriculture and manufacturing interests from our districts, the chair of the Oregon State University Graduate School Environmental Sciences Department and a regional administrator from the Oregon State Department of Environmental Quality. The journey of what was officially titled the "Oregon Legislative Friendship and Trade Delegation," took 16 days and included visits to eight cities, and a Sustainable Economic Development Seminar (the first such seminar held with China), a mini-trade show of Oregon products, an opening reception for Jepsen—our recently hired trade consultant—and a tour of grass seed demonstration project in Shanghai.

The delegation's trip came at a particularly opportune time, as Chinese leaders were beginning to commit large financial resources to improve their country's infamously polluted environment. Oregon is a state that is justifiably proud of our reputation as a "green" state, and I believed that our expertise in this area would lead to increased economic connections, exchange of technology, and would yield immeasurable benefits for both Oregon and China. One of the highlights of the trip was the signing of a Memorandum of Understanding with the Fujian province, which guaranteed the display of Oregon products in their International Exhibition Center at a discount fee, and made arrangements for local contractors to manage the sales of Oregon products in the province and elsewhere in China.

An especially proud moment for me occurred during the visit with State Senate President Brady Adams presented a scholarship for two years of graduate study leading to a master's degree in urban studies or environmental science at Oregon's Portland State University. The full tuition scholarship also included a $5,000 contribution to room and board over the two years of study, which Senate President Adams announced was given by "Senator Mae Yih, who is a bridge between Oregon and China." A similar scholarship was given to the Fujian province in our sister state. I made this contribution to further strengthen better understanding and the bonds of co-operation and learning between China and Oregon.

As usual, it took a great deal of preparation to arrange the trip, but as we returned to the United States, I was very proud of all that had been accomplished and grateful for the kind words of my legislative colleagues and the business leaders who thanked me for such a successful and productive visit. They were impressed with the fast growth of China's economy everywhere we went, the warmth expressed in their receptions and sumptuous banquets, and the rich culture and history of China. Most interestingly, my legislative colleagues and business delegates observed that China was more market oriented, while the United States was bogged down with process when we can't even utilize our own resources for production. They were rightfully concerned about the United States' ability to compete in the global market.

The delegation's compliments about the success of the trip made it all the more surprising when, upon our return from China, my staff shared with me an *Oregonian* article that had been printed while we were gone, and quoted officials from the OECDD who questioned the value of the trip and my leadership of it. This article only served to increase my incredible frustration with the OECDD. As I planned the 2000 trip to China—and many of the trips before it—I was invariably disappointed by the department's complete inability to understand the importance of China as a trading partner, and their lack of response to my requests for assistance and information.

At each point in the planning of the 2000 trip, I suggested ways in which they might be of assistance to the delegation—which, after all, included the top three members of the Senate leadership—but my requests were routinely ignored or delayed.

For example, when I asked them to send out invitations to Oregon environmental protection and high tech companies that might be interested in participating in the Sustainable Economic Development Seminar or the trip, they only did so just four weeks before the trip began. This short notice did not allow business executives, engineers or scientists enough time to plan for participation at the seminar, apply for a visa, or to make the arrangements necessary to be gone sixteen days. OECDD should have sent out the notices at least four months before the trip. After all, the Sustainable Economic Development Seminar was suggested by the Assistant Director of OECDD to the Vice Mayor of Shanghai in November, 1999 and Oregon's signing of a memorandum of understanding in April, 1999 with the Chinese Minister of Science and Technology establishing in Oregon a China-U.S. Center for Sustainable Development (CUCSD) was by the Director of OECDD. The Governor's International Trade Policy Statement dated Jan. 3, 2000 emphasized the importance of promoting export business stating that one out of five jobs in Oregon is a direct result of international trade and investment. It was obviously OECDD's responsibility to carry out their director and assistant director's commitment and implement the governor's international trade policy and directives. Further, OECDD insinuated that the only reason the businesses that joined the trip were invited was because they were contributors to legislative campaigns. This was a slap in the face to the integrity of all the legislators on the trip.

And when OECDD finally did indicate interest in sending a staff member on the trip, it was someone who did not speak Chinese, and would not have been able to make any meaningful contribution. It is common knowledge that one has to be able to read and write Chinese in order to be able to at least pronounce names correctly and not confuse last names with first names, not to mention to be able to interpret businesses and technical matters accurately. Senate President Adams and I had to do desperate last minute recruitment for an environmental protection scientist and consultant to participate in the Sustainable Economic Development Seminar so that Oregon would not become the laughing stock of the world to have the seminar without any experts from Oregon on the panel due to lack of response and cooperation from OECDD. President Adams and I both sighed a deep sigh of relief four weeks before departure, when we were able to recruit the chair of the Oregon State University Graduate School Environmental Sciences Department and the regional administrator from the Oregon Department of Environmental Quality to join the trip and the seminar, instead of waiting for OECDD, who was unable and unwilling to fulfill their responsibility.

My frustration with the OECDD only increased further when, shortly after returning from the trip, I received a letter from Don Alanen in Beaverton, who sympathized with me after reading the Oregonian article of OECDD official criticizing me for being overly demanding in the arrangement of the Seminar and the Legislative Trade Delegation's business appointments and trip schedule. Mr. Alanen detailed the difficult experience he had when he attempted to set up an International Trade Fair with China in Portland. The OECDD refused to support his trade fair, which led to his bank refusing to provide financing for the two-day event.

During my final legislative session in 2001, I succeeded in bringing some much needed reform and accountability to the OECDD. This was the result of an audit I had requested from the Oregon Secretary of State's office in 2000. I asked that office to review and evaluate the reliability and validity of the OECDD's performance measurement system. Since 1993, the department had been required by statute to deliver biennial reports to the Governor and the Legislative assembly on the success of their economic development efforts. Not surprisingly, the April 2001 audit revealed some glaring weaknesses in the OECDD, including the fact that the department had unclear objectives, weak performance measures, a lack of comparisons, and unreliable data. The department's job reports were verified to be correct in only 3 out of 19 cases.

This audit report verified my concerns over the ineffectiveness and lack of accountability at OECDD, and led directly to the overwhelming passage of legislation that directed the Legislative Fiscal Office to enter into a contract with an independent consultant to evaluate the cost effectiveness of OECDD and to recommend improvements in state funded programs that were designed to promote the creation of jobs.

During my final legislative session in 2001, I also took action to ensure that the partnerships between Oregon and China that I had helped to build during my legislative service would continue when I retired from public office. I did this by co-authoring legislation recommended by former Senate President Brady Adams, who led the Legislative Friendship and Trade Delegation in 1997 and 2000 that established a privately funded biennial trade delegation consisting of legislative leaders and business representatives that would continue to promote and enhance friendly cultural and trade relations with Oregon's sister state, Fujian province. The bill had a very minimal fiscal impact, but its effect on long term economic growth and improved relations would be major.

My efforts to build a strong relationship between Oregon and Asia were enthusiastically supported by my constituents in a very personal way. In 1994, I helped arrange a Linn County visit by a large delegation from Shitara, Japan. Shitara was a small town with a population of 6,200, which was nestled in the mountains of central Japan, about 130 miles west of Tokyo. Shitara's main industries were forest products, rice, tomatoes and cabbage. The Mayor of Shitara was Yoneharu Goto, who, as a young man, spent eight months on a coastal Oregon dairy farm. He had organized the trip through Oregon's trade office in Japan, telling them he was looking for an area with an economy similar to Shitara's. The trade office contacted me to help and I consented. Mayor Goto hoped the visit would help to stimulate interest in forest products and agriculture and end a steady decline in Shitara's population.

The Shitara delegation, led by Mayor Goto, included 63 ninth graders and 16 adult chaperones, including school principals, teachers and parents of students. I went to the Linn County schools and the county Extension Service and asked them to provide names of families with children in the 4-H program who might be willing to host the visiting ninth graders in their homes for two days and three nights. I was delighted when 32 families volunteered. The experience was so successful that it was repeated again the very next summer when 67 middle school students and 16 adult chaperones from Shitara arrived in Albany for a two-day visit. Once again, I worked closely with city and school officials, 4-H leaders, and interested citizens to arrange housing and special events for the delegation. Among their many stops were a tour of a grass seed farm, a grass seed laboratory, a pulp and paper mill, a mobile home manufacturing plant, and a community picnic. I am sure that the highlight of the trip for the students was a visit to the Oregon State Fair in Salem.

Amidst all the fun and good memories of these visits was a serious purpose: by highlighting Oregon's agriculture and timber industries to young students, we were fostering a very important two-way exchange that would benefit both Oregon and Japan. I also want to share that at the end of the 1995 visit, one of the parent representatives gave me an envelope and told me it was from Mayor Goto. I immediately placed the unopened envelope in the leather folder I always carried with me and didn't think any more of it as I continued with my busy schedule. That evening, I opened the envelope and discovered much to my shock that it contained 20 U.S. one hundred dollar bills— a total of $2,000! I assume the Japanese parents thought that the money was a gift to thank me for helping to arrange the exchange program. Legislators, of course, are banned from accepting personal cash gifts under any circumstances, and I quickly wrote to Mayor Goto, explaining that fact and telling him that the money would be used to create a scholarship account for teachers and students involved in the program.

That exchange continued in the summer of 1996, when I was delighted to accept Mayor Goto's invitation to lead a delegation of Oregon students, educators and parents on a trip to Shitara. The eleven-member Oregon delegation stayed with local host families during the three-day, four-night visit, and the students who made the trip were able to stay with the Japanese students that they had hosted during their Oregon visit. I was invited to stay at the home of Shitara Mayor Yoneharu Goto. It was a very unique experience, to say the least. The Mayor and his wife lived in an old house with a big vegetable garden. My bedroom—which contained no furniture except for a flat mattress on the floor and a desk by the window—was in an attic near their living room. I had to climb a ten-step ladder to get to my room. There was no light in the attic except a bulb hanging on a wire from the ceiling. There was also no chair in my room, so I had to sit on my mat to write my diary, and I sat on a desk by the window to put on my makeup. And if I needed to visit the bathroom at night, I would have to take a flashlight, climb down the ladder, walk through a dirt alley to the kitchen, and walk through another dirt alley to the bathroom—which had no sink. I had to brush my teeth in the shower or via the kitchen faucet. I had to face mosquito bites during the night, since the home had a big garden and was near a creek. The Mayor did present me with an honorary citizenship award for my work in the student exchange program, plus the incredibly warm hospitality of the people and the Drum Festival was so breathtakingly outstanding that I suppose I shouldn't complain!

While in Shitara, the Oregon delegation participated in day-long festival which featured a parade and drum, martial arts, and folk dancing performances. The performances were enhanced by the use of traditional costumes, including devil masks, wooden spears and Samurai warrior uniforms of 500 years ago. The beating of large drums, exotic devils' masks, colorful costumes and theatrical dance and acts seemed like scenes from an exhilarating movie. We also took part in a Samurai parade where all the elementary students wore homemade warrior costumes. This was all part of a Drum Festival where the natives pay homage to the ancestors using drums and dancing. The Buddhist festival parade ended at the temple, where seven adult samurai in full costume pay their respects at the grave of the town's most famous samurai, while a Buddhist monk chants and rings bells. The festival began with the parade at 11:00 in the morning and didn't end until a fireworks demonstration at 10:00 in the evening. The eleven-hour celebration was a very memorable day for the entire Oregon delegation. Other highlights of the trip included the Shitara Friendship Club presenting the delegation with "Happy Coats," teaching us how to make rice sweet cake by mallet pounding, learning how to catch live fish with our bare hands, and a delicious barbecue lunch featuring a variety of meat, vegetables, seafood, and homemade soba noodles that were eaten with cold soup and special gluttonous rice pastry.

The delegation also visited summer schools and toured the ancient cities of Kyoto and Tokyo. Wherever we went, we couldn't help but notice the wonderful tradition of families taking care of aged parents. Mayor Goto and his wife lived with his 82 year-old mother, and the family across the street from the Mayor had an 89 year-old father living with them.

When the trip was completed and we returned to Oregon, it was clear that the students, parents, and teachers who traveled to Shitara had built warmer friendships and deeper understanding of Japanese people, and were better prepared to do business with and teach others about one of our most important international neighbors. It was truly a grass roots exchange.

The exchange program continued in the summer of 1997, 1998, 1999, 2000, 2001, and 2002 when delegations of students, teachers, principals, and parent chaperones and city officials from Shitara traveled to Linn County. Also in July of 1998, a separate delegation of farmers from Shitara led again by Mayor Goto spent several days in Linn County to observe Albany's Timber Carnival festivities followed by a tour of a local dairy. This was the first adult-only delegation from Shitara, and their visit sent a strong message of the importance of international trade, tourism and friendship. The exchange program continued for nine years until my retirement from the Legislature, when I returned the accumulated scholarship cash fund in the amount of $14,525 to Mayor Goto, so that the program could be continued under a different sponsorship.

I was very touched recently when grandson Christopher chose to write a school paper during his sophomore year in Dartmouth College about Chinese immigrants, and my life and legislative service. Christopher did a great deal of research in writing his 29-page paper, and he was especially curious about my efforts in forging friendship and economic ties between Oregon and China. In his paper, he gave my efforts credit for helping to increase Oregon exports to China from $36 million annually in 1989 to over $640 million annually in 2003.

I am proud to close this chapter by sharing some of Christopher's writing:

"One of the most prominent displays of Mae's effectiveness concerned the issue of trade liberalization and China. In an almost cyclical turn to her childhood experience in Shanghai, in 1997 Mae sponsored a bill to increase trade negotiations with China. Mae recognized the immense trade opportunity in the Chinese markets, remembering the great period of industrialization that marked her father's success in the early 20th century...In 1997, when Mae first introduced the bill, China was ranked as Oregon's twenty-first trading partner—far below other industrial Asian nations like Japan, Taiwan, and South Korea. Mae, remembering her childhood and recognizing the ample opportunity in the Chinese market, fought to establish an Oregon trade office in Shanghai. China's growing markets seemed like the perfect consumer for Oregon's lumber and agricultural products.

Mae faced incredible opposition among other Representatives and Senators. Many opponents called into question China's vast corruption, human rights violations, and flagrant disregard for international cooperation and diplomacy...Many of the Oregon legislators were still apprehensive to engage in trade negotiations with the Chinese government...Thinking back to her childhood in Shanghai, Mae could not shake the memory of seeing the dead bodies wrapped in straw mats on the street. She reflected, "Americans do not understand or underestimate the extreme poverty in China. Survival comes before individual rights. Do you want a bowl of rice or the ability to vote? As standard of living increases, people will be more concerned with individual rights. Lifting of people out of extreme poverty is critical in building strength and health of the nation before democracy can be restored. We both have problems. Let's support common goals." Mae continued to press the Oregon legislature to help increase the Chinese standard of living instead of questioning their politics and governance.

"As one of Mae's major accomplishments during her long career of public service, Oregon-China trade continues to stand as a testament to the legacy of Mae Yih from Shanghai to Albany, Oregon. Mae's career of public service has both responded to the concerns of her American constituency and increased economic developments back in China. As a literal coming together of China and Oregon, these trade negotiations symbolically represent how one woman used her immigrant experience to change the lives of millions of people on both sides of the Pacific Ocean.

Mae's life story reveals the untold narrative of a Chinese woman on the frontier of American society. In her process of becoming more American, she has aided in the centuries long struggle to make America a little more Chinese. In shedding light on this history, I hope that we continue to change and recognize the story of the Chinese in the United States as not a foreign story, but as a quintessentially American one. One that tells the story of devastation, immigration, hard work, and success. In striving to redefine what it means to be American, Mae has opened up a world of possibility for new immigrants. From stepping off the boat in San Francisco to the floor of the Oregon State Legislature, Mae's life uncovers a wealth of immigrant and American history. In her journey from Shanghai to Oregon, she has come into direct contact with the intermixing worlds of global industrialization and trade, Chinese communism, global capitalism, American nationalism, and civil rights activism. Her story reveals one thoroughly of the 20th century, with the downfall of colonialism, the rise of radical extremism, Cold War politics, and surges in new international migration patterns. Yet her story also speaks to an older narrative of Chinese in the United States, the forgotten coal miners and railroad workers of Gumshan (Gold Mountain) and the American West, and how American views of the Chinese have changed and not changed since their first arrival."

Christopher also astutely pointed out that while Chinese immigrants have made much progress in the United States, there is still work to be done in combatting discrimination and stereotypes. He wrote:

"Yet, with all her success and all her determination, we do not see a story complete. Contemporary stereotypes of Chinese Americans painfully bind and limit their futures and success in this country. The downtown Chinese and their limited social mobility are evidence of this phenomenon. Even with the success of people like Mae and Washington Governor Gary Locke, Chinese Americans must still continually dawn the racial uniform that marks their heritage and status as outsiders. Anti-Chinese backlash that has emerged as a response to the global rise of Chinese military and economic power has led to severe calls for the internment of all Chinese Americans and/or the deportation of the Chinese American community. Even with the great strides of Chinese American politicians, intellectuals, artists, writers, industrialists, and laborers, the story of the Chinese in America is still not over and done."

I agree with Christopher's observation that racial discrimination and bias against Chinese Americans still exists and can be seen in two recent actions by the federal government against two China-born naturalized citizens.

In 2014, Sherry Chen, an Ohio-based hydrologist for the National Weather Service, was accused of being a Chinese mole. She was charged with four felonies, including unlawfully downloading information about critical infrastructure. The prosecution began after a colleague reported that she had e-mailed an official at China's Ministry of Water Resources. The e-mail was actually Ms. Chen's response to a question from a Chinese official who had asked her during a meeting in Beijing how water infrastructure projects in America were funded. The information she sent him was harmless and publicly available.

And in 2015, federal prosecutors brought charges against Dr. Xi Xiao Xing, the chairman of the physics department at Temple University in Philadelphia. Dr. Xi was accused of sharing privileged technology with China by providing the design of a pocket heater that was used in superconductor research—a charge that carried a punishment of up to 80 years in prison. Charges were eventually dropped when Dr. Xi's defense lawyers pointed out that the information he e-mailed scientists in China was completely unrelated to the pocket heater.

Though the charges against both Ms. Chen and Dr. Xi were eventually dropped, the initial accusations traumatized them and their families and damaged their professional reputations. Neither received a much-deserved apology from the federal government.

These and other examples of racial profiling and discrimination are not acceptable and need to be investigated, explained and apologized by the United States Department of Justice and the victims should be properly compensated. Guidelines for factual and careful investigation in similar cases also need to be established to avoid future wrongful accusations and racial discrimination. It is possible to prevent the stealing of America's classified and proprietary information, and simultaneously protect the rights of all American citizens. America must always remain the "land of the free and the home of the brave."

CHAPTER 5: **2002: My final year in public office**

Of my 26 years in the Oregon State Legislature, one of the busiest and most eventful was 2002—my final year in elective office, and a year that deserves its own chapter.

I had decided in 2001 that I would not seek re-election in 2002 to a sixth term in the Oregon State Senate. It wasn't that I was tired of the work—I still enjoyed it and felt that I was responding faithfully and successfully to constituents' concerns for the benefit of the community, state, and country.

But I was 74 years old, and I would be 78 years old at the end of a sixth term. I had also missed out on spending time with my husband, sons, and with you, my grandsons. It was time to put family ahead of public service. Speaking of family, I was very proud to have so many family members, including my two sons and all my handsome grandsons travel to Albany in March 2002 to attend an Albany Chamber of Commerce banquet where I was honored for my 39 years in public service. All those who attended heard Senator Cliff Trow, my long time legislative colleague from Corvallis, say that I "worked tirelessly to find inefficiencies in state government, demanded that agencies meet performance goals, and labored long hours for her constituents."

In my remarks that evening, I briefly shared my coming from China and spoke about the debt I owed America. I concluded by stressing my firm belief that everyone needed to be involved in strengthening and maintaining democracy and keeping our country strong. I also encouraged the audience to run for elected office, reminding them that if an unknown, foreign-born housewife could be elected to the legislature, so could they! "This is America," I said. "It's a land of freedom and unlimited opportunities, and if you set your mind to it, you will succeed!"

I received a preview of retirement in the summer of 2002 when Steve and I joined grandson Stephen on a seven day Alaskan cruise in celebration of Stephen's 10th birthday. I hope you have as many good memories of the trip as I do, Stephen! I still recall the beautiful scenery of the ice glaciers floating in the ocean, and of following you as you ran from the ship's first floor all the way to the fourth floor and back to the first floor. I also remember visiting excavated gold mines, taking a helicopter tour of the glaciers, attending a whale watch, having a fresh barbecued salmon picnic, and eating lots of ice cream as a special treat for you! Following the Alaskan cruise, the whole family met in Whistler, British Columbia for a week to celebrate Steve's 80th birthday. Whistler was great fun with activities for everyone from bungee jumping to horseback riding.

Since I was retiring from the legislature in January 2003, I worked diligently throughout 2002 to ensure that the causes and issues for which I fought would not go away after I was gone from Salem and no one paid attention to me anymore!

I also used my last year in the legislature to reinforce the importance of a strong friendly relationship between Oregon and China, organizing and making arrangements for a friendship and trade legislative delegation to China in May, 2002. The 21-member delegation included the two top legislative leaders—Senate President Gene Derfler and Speaker of the House Mark Simmons—as well as Senators Jason Atkinson and Margaret Carter, Representatives Bob Jenson, Al King, three family members of legislators, and Tom Brian, a former legislator who was serving as Chair of the Washington County Commission, and ten representatives from small and medium sized businesses and higher education institutions in our legislative districts. The presence of Senate President Derfler and House Speaker Simmons led to some long-distance phone calls as they discussed the state's worsening budget problems with Governor Kitzhaber. The Governor had proposed that they not make the trip, but Derfler and Simmons correctly concluded that it would cause a loss of credibility and business opportunities. "The best way out of this recession is to create jobs," Derfler said. "We expect that our meetings in China will be beneficial to Oregon businesses." Speaker Simmons also pointed out that in Oregon, one of every five jobs was directly tied to international trade.

As with past delegation trips to China, I devoted a lot of time in planning a trip that would be informational and constructive. Here, in greater detail, is a summary of the six-city May 22-June 4 trip:

One of the highlights of the mission was a meeting in Beijing with then Vice Premier Wen Jia Pao, who was destined to be the next premier of China, and Foreign Minister Li Zhao Xing. The Vice Premier managed agriculture, finance and sustainable development issues for the Chinese government. He was very well versed regarding Oregon, and even mentioned the Oregon Trail and famed Oregon pioneer John McLoughlin. He was also extremely interested in establishing a 5 million-hectare greenbelt around China. We discussed a variety of sustainable development projects, including a gift by delegation member and nursery owner Bob Terry of a sustainable development park designed for the 2008 Summer Olympic games.

Another highlight was traveling to the Xinjiang province, which borders the Gobi Desert, to investigate the potential of a joint project involving research and planting of drought-tolerant varieties of vegetation. The plants would also be used later in other parts of Western China for environmental protection by reclaiming the desert land with trees and grasses. This was similar to Vice Premier Wen's goal of establishing a greenbelt. These environmental projects were critical given that Beijing had faced dust storms twelve times during the previous spring. Such storms had only occurred two or three times during the entire decade of the 1970's.

While in Xinjiang, we were hosted by Provincial leaders to a banquet of unique native food, including camel's paw garnished with a huge heap of whipped egg white. While bear paw is considered the most elite of all gourmet foods in China, camel's paw is a close second. Everyone had a good time drinking "fire water," which was 100% proof liquor—everyone that is except for the OSU Forestry Department professor, who refused because of dietary reasons, and me! As you know, I don't drink a drop of liquor, since my father always told me that Chinese women don't drink.

The delegation then went to Turpan, an ancient city in Xinjiang province, which is their "grape valley" and also known as the raisin capital of China. Their raisins are twice as large as our raisins, green in color, and very sweet. If I were a businessperson, I would go into the business of importing these raisins to America. We also saw small grape-drying huts along the fields that were made of mud bricks with spaces between every other brick to enhance drying and ventilation under the hot sun. (It was 97 degrees during our visit!) We also visited farmers' homes, watched the native women dance, and were invited to participate in the dance with them. It was a great deal of fun!

We then flew to Dunhuang in Gansu province, where we had lunch with the leaders of the Dunhuang People's Congress. We took in sightseeing in the afternoon at the base of the Singing Sand Mountain, where we had two-hump camel rides, sand dune slides, and home cooked dinner by local farmers featuring soya sauce/wine chicken with red dates. While we ate, we also enjoyed listening to a local orchestra playing music on native musical instruments. We also went to a night market, where I bought six small snuff tobacco glass bottles with painting on the inside of the bottles. The price was 5 yuans each—about U.S. sixty cents each. After we returned to Oregon, one of the delegation members told me they were avoiding me at the tourists' camel ride and sand dune slides because I was pressuring them to do what I did—to be adventurous and try the rides and slides. I enjoyed them very much.

The delegation next flew to Chengdu, capital of the Sichuan province, where we had a discussion about a possible joint venture in grass seed production. We also visited the Giant Panda Research Center, where everyone had their photograph taken with a baby panda at the cost of U.S. $50 each. The delegation members loved it. I didn't have a picture taken since I already had one taken with a "movie star" giant panda at Yaan City near Chengdu during my last visit there in October 2000. U.S.Consulate General David Bleyle in Chengdu gave the delegation a warm reception in the evening.

It was then off to Yichang city in Hubei province, where we were amazed by the tremendous engineering work of the Three Gorges Dam. We also inspected the grass seed demonstration plots from Oregon that was being tested for use on hundreds of miles of river banks to prevent soil erosion and the subsequent build up of silt in the Yangtze River. Grass seed had rapidly become one of Oregon's most important exports to China, with a phenomenal 6,900% increase in just five years. The delegation then left for Shanghai, where we enjoyed a delightful lunch (including escargot cooked in the French style) hosted by the Shanghai branch of the Portland based law firm, Davis, Wright, and Tremaine.

Following lunch, we visited the Shanghai Institute for International Studies, where we listened to a presentation on human rights and Taiwan. In the evening, we walked on Nanking Road, Shanghai's busy business district, where we visited the prominent 200 room Palace Hotel. I thought of my father, who was the owner of the Palace Hotel after World War II, during the heyday of his success. At that time, it was a symbol of Shanghai, which was known as the "Pearl of the Orient."

While in Shanghai, before we left to return to Oregon, I sent out surveys to delegation members, asking for comments and ideas for future improvements and wrote my trip news release so that I could have the legislative leaders review it during our return plane ride. A delicious lunch was hosted by Wu Jing Song, Director of the Shanghai Environmental Protection Bureau Planning Division, where we discussed the fact that one of their officials was taking a two year graduate study program in environmental protection at Portland State University, due to the Senate President Brady Adams Scholarship Fund that I had sponsored in 2000. The official was to return to China in the spring of 2003, when she could be most helpful in coordinating joint projects or starting new ventures. In the afternoon, we visited the Yu Garden, a large shopping center that was built on the ground of an old imperial residence and garden. It was a great idea to use the old ornate buildings for shops and restaurants, while preserving as a scenic and historic attraction the beautifully landscaped garden of stone hills, ponds, nine curved bridges and carved dragon walls. Delegation members bought a lot of cultured pearls and jade necklaces.

Dinner was hosted by officials from the Fujian province, our sister state, who were most thoughtful of our tight schedule and the fact that we were unable to visit their province as we needed to get back to Oregon to deal with the budget crisis. On the morning before we took off for Hong Kong to begin our return to the United States, we visited the nursery and wood product market with delegation members Bob Terry and Jim Prouchnau, guided by Fujian province representatives in forestry and the new Pudong area. I treated the whole delegation for lunch at the Seagull restaurant. We also visited the Oriental Pearl Television Tower, and went for a Disneyland-like tunnel ocean ride in the afternoon. We flew to Hong Kong in the late afternoon and returned home to Oregon on June 4.

Survey comments from delegation members were returned to me before we made the long flight home, and they were very helpful to me. Their comments included:

*Concerns with environmental protection and sustainability, both in air and water quality. In spite of much propaganda and some progress in the larger cities, there was considerable evidence that China had a long way to go. Coal burning was everywhere, as was soil erosion. China only has sewage treatment for 1/3 of its population, and had not yet addressed non-point pollution.

* Opportunities in agriculture and forestry could be immediate, but China was not ready to accept help or pay the cost of environmental protection at a rate faster than they are currently funding. The economic benefits to some business sectors were obvious.

* In the future, we should provide better details on stop sites, potential costs, and what is expected to be accomplished prior to the trip.

* Don't try to see too many places, as we moved too many times.

* Improving trust and friendly relationship between the U.S. and China would allow free trade. Long-term relationships grow long-term business, which would grow Oregon's economy. Improvement in global peace could also be derived.

After we returned from the trip, upon careful consideration of our observations of their needs and interests, in consultation with delegation member Dr. Robert Rose of the OSU Forestry Department, I asked Senate President Derfler and House Speaker Simmons to join me in writing to Abudureyimu Amiti, Deputy Director of the Regional People's Congress of Xinjiang province, who hosted the delegation during our visit, to invite them to visit Oregon with a technical team to show them our university, forest and grass seed industries. During the visit we could also discuss the possibilities of joint research in a green belt plan for protection and development of pastureland and prevention of further expansion of the desert. We envisioned a ten-year cooperative project. We explained that we were enthusiastic about the possible cooperative project and we deeply appreciated their warm hospitality during our visit. I also wrote twelve additional letters on behalf of the delegation, thanking our various hosts.

A few months after returning from China, the delegation re-united in Salem for a committee hearing and brown-bag lunch where we reported on the details and accomplishments of the trip. We took the opportunity to make the point that as a leader in high-tech, agricultural, forest products and environmental protection services, coupled with our close geographical proximity to China, Oregon remained uniquely situated to expand our export market to China and to create jobs. We stressed that it was very important for Oregon's governor, legislators, and businesses to maintain regular visits with Chinese leaders and officials, as doors and opportunities tended to open for our businesses.

Dr. Rose was invited to make a Power Point presentation on the trip and the lessons we learned. He made note of the fact that forested land in China accounted for only about 13% of total land area, in comparison to 43% of forested land in the United States. Dr. Rose advocated for strong reforestation efforts in China, and recommended the need to establish a long-range plan of a five million- hectare greenbelt around China, as was pointed out by Vice Premier Wen Jia Pao during our meeting with him in Beijing. Dr. Rose also offered to fund a tuition-free scholarship with monthly stipends for Chinese students. He concluded that an Oregon demonstration project during the 2008 Olympic Games would be a superb way to "sell" Oregon to the world.

As an aside from the topic of China, Dr. Rose also made a very good suggestion about economic development in Oregon that I have remembered ever since. He said that brick and mortar have not worked well when it comes to building intellectual power. "Mind power comes from spending $20 million on faculty with reputations and ability," he said. The same point was made to me by Ralph Shaw, the Chair of the Governor's Economic Advisory Council, who during hearings recommended that more money should be spent in the Oregon State University engineering school in attracting world-class professors, in scholarships for talented and motivated students from around the world, and in internships with high-tech companies. Mr. Shaw was concerned with the very small amount of patents that were coming out of Oregon's engineering schools compared to those coming out of Washington and other states, thereby exacerbating the stagnant stage of Oregon's high-tech industry.

I am very pleased to report that Oregon Governor Kate Brown led a delegation to China in the fall of 2015. Governor Brown first visited China as part of the friendship and trade mission I helped to organize when she was Senate Minority Leader in 2000. I am also proud of the fact that the Oregon Economic and Community Development Department (now called "Business Oregon," still maintains a trade representative based in China.) Finally, I am especially delighted to report that according to the April 2016 Portland Business Journal, the value of Oregon exports to China in 2015 was nearly $4.5 billion, making it our state's largest export destination. The bottom line is that all my twenty-four years of efforts to build friendship and to forge economic ties between Oregon and China which began in 1979 when I invited Ron Yi Ren, the Chairman of the China International Trust and Investment Corporation, to visit Oregon and meet with Governor Atiyeh, legislators and business leaders ended up in making a very positive difference for both my beloved native and adopted countries.

My chief focus in 2002, however, was what was always my top priority—restoring people's faith in government through high performance by full accountability of spending and meeting performance measures in all state agencies. This focus was more important than ever in 2002, as the poor economy had put the state in a budget crisis that required an unprecedented five special sessions of the legislature.

As the legislature convened for the first special session in March, I proposed a modified budget freeze as the best way to put our financial house in order and to address the budget shortfall. I saw the recession and the budget crisis as a great opportunity to eliminate inefficient programs, duplications, and reduce bureaucracy. My proposal called for no salary increases for any state employee, no increase in the number of government agency staff, and no new state programs until the economy recovered. I wish I could report that my legislative colleagues agreed that we should not spend money that we didn't have and that they supported my proposal, but I was told by the chairman of the special senate budget committee that I would only get three votes. Instead, the legislature passed a plan that balanced the budget partially by taking more than $200 million from a lottery funded education endowment fund that Oregon voters had approved in 1995. The legislative plan required voters to approve the "borrowing" of the education endowment fund in a May 2002 election. I strongly opposed the plan, pointing out that 75% of the interest earnings from the fund were used to pay off school construction bonds and to support college scholarships for needy students. To strip money from those programs would harm future generations by putting Oregon further into debt. The voters of Oregon agreed with me, as they defeated the legislative proposal in the May election. The legislature then was called back into session to find another way to balance the budget.

As the months dragged on, the recession deepened, and Oregon's budget deficit grew ever larger. Governor Kitzhaber proposed a package of tax increases, which I strongly opposed. Oregon had the highest unemployment rate in the nation, and increasing personal and corporate income taxes would only mean less consumer consumption, less money for business investment, further increasing unemployment and prolonging the recession. Many legislators supported a plan that included across the board cuts in funding which would result in cutting funding for schools, police, and early release of prisoners. I argued that instead we should eliminate lower priority programs and use the savings to preserve essential services that we were elected to provide to the citizens of our state for their safety and welfare. I submitted a 10-point list of $490.5 million in funding reductions of low-priority programs and adopting several ideas for cuts and efficiency measures recommended by senate colleagues and the state auditor. For example, I proposed abolishing the Criminal Justice Commission and using its $19 million in funding to prevent the state police from having to eliminate 131 state troopers and 50 support staff. I also proposed privatizing management of prisons, selling state motor pool cars that were not being used efficiently, and a variety of other low-priority program reductions.

I also used the special sessions as an opportunity to again point out the lack of performance of the Oregon Economic and Community Development Department. There could be no doubt that the facts were in my favor: Since its establishment in 1973, the OECDD had spent $2.7 billion. Their annual budget had grown almost 300 times from $1.7 million to $473 million, and their full time employees had increased almost sevenfold, from 22 to 149. And what did this money get for Oregon? Well, we had the highest unemployment rate in the nation, the highest hunger rate in the nation, and Oregon's per capita income compared to the U.S. average had dropped from 101.4% to 93%. The mission of the OECDD was to create jobs, but a consultant's study found that only 20% of the Department's projects were targeted to job creation, and a state audit concluded that only 3 out of the 19 projects OECDD reported were accurate in the number of jobs created. The bottom line, I argued, was that it would be more cost effective to eliminate the department, and use the savings of $473 million to balance the budget and save essential state programs. Job creation and the promotion of business and trade would be left in the capable hands of private enterprise with less over-regulation and red tape from government.

The 2001 Legislature had passed a bill that I sponsored requiring an independent study of OECDD's economic development programs and recommendations for improvement of the cost effectiveness of its programs. The report was to be presented to the 2003 legislature. To keep the ball rolling, I chaired a hearing in April 2002 where I invited Dr. William Conerly, Chair of the Cascade Policy Institute to testify. The invitation was prompted by Conerly's 1995 report, "The Unseen Costs of Ribbon Cutting:

Losses from Economic Development Programs." The key recommendation of the paper was the elimination of the Oregon Economic and Community Development Department. He wrote "Government support for economic development programs replaces the discipline of the market with the judgment of politicians and bureaucrats."

After the hearing, I proposed a committee draft to restructure Oregon Economic Development by reducing the department to 13 employees: six employees in the Governor's office to concentrate on international trade, business recruitment and problem solving; and seven employees in the Housing Division to process infrastructure and business loans. Many small businesses testified in support of the idea of eliminating the department because it did not help them. Grants and loans had been awarded that created unfair competition, and department rules and regulations were overly restrictive. We also heard suggestions about the need to stimulate high-tech industries and establishing "shovel ready" industrial sites.

While the committee draft plan was a good one, I confess that in the back of my mind, I really wanted to propose cutting the OECDD to only two staff members in the Governor's office, as had been recommended by Dr. Conerly. One of the staff members could assist businesses in getting permits and licenses, and the other could refer any business inquiries to local economic development officers.

Unfortunately, I could not convince the Senate Budget Committee to approve the subcommittee's proposal to restructure the Department. I finally proposed a scaled back Senate Resolution, which was adopted by the Committee and passed by the Senate during the Special Session. Senate Joint Resolution 4 aimed to make the state Economic and Community Development Department more accountable and efficient through increased reporting and oversight. It urged OECDD to improve its efficiency and report any progress using "verifiable and accurate" data from the Employment Department and not just estimates. It asked the agency to submit strategies for reducing the regulations for business permits and improving the quality and quantity of high-tech investment opportunities. The resolution also asked the Department to publish the costs to benefit ratio of each of its programs so "legislators and taxpayers can understand the advantages and disadvantages of each."

I took advantage of one more opportunity to point out the failures of the Oregon Economic and Community Development Department at a Leadership Summit in Portland in December 2002 called by U.S. Senator Ron Wyden and then Governor-elect Ted Kulongoski. The Summit was attended by over 500 government and business leaders. I testified and handed out a report containing the statistics I cited during the special sessions that highlighted the high cost and lack of results of the OECDD. I urged the leaders to take a few minutes to review and digest the numbers and to consider that at the time, Oregon had the highest unemployment rate in the nation for 14 of the previous 16 months, and that despite the fact that Oregon was a strong agricultural state, our hunger rate was highest in the nation. I suggested that the leaders honestly ask themselves if the Oregon Economic Development Department was effective? I appreciated the calling of a summit in shaping Oregon's economic future, as I believed it offered an opportune time to pause and take a good hard look at what was the most cost-effective way to promote our economy. I urged the formation of a small task force of successful business leaders and academics and charging them with submitting a proposal that would reduce or eliminate the OECDD, and that would result in high employment and a prosperous economy for Oregon.

One of the frustrations of the special session was that even in the midst of a budget crisis, the Legislature refused to deal with the issue of a skyrocketing public employee retirement system (PERS). The overly generous system actually paid the average employee who retired after 30 years of public service 105% of his or her final salary. This system was threatening to bankrupt many local governments. Despite this, legislation to reform the PERS system failed on a 15-15 vote. As I write this in 2015, high PERS costs continue to severely impact the budgets of state and local governments. Had the legislature had the foresight to pass the PERS reform in 2002, many problems could have been avoided.

Another frustration of the session-and for many of my legislative sessions—was that whenever state agencies were instructed to reduce spending, they would report back with plans that slashed essential services, which would lead to a public uproar. I argued that state agencies needed to prioritize and eliminate low priority non-essential services, duplications, bureaucracy, and red tape, and that they should implement cost savings and efficiency measures. After all, Oregonians did that at home and in business when revenue declined and we should apply the same logic to government. I said, "If we take out the wants, preserve the needs, and live within our income, we will go a long way in gaining the public's faith and trust in government and speeding the recovery of the health of our economy."

In fact, I believe that there could have been a silver lining in the budget crisis: It forced us to carefully scrutinize our state government programs to weed out inefficiencies and streamline structure to improve productivity. After all, as policy makers, our most important responsibility was to be held accountable to the citizens of our state, and the best way to do that was to constantly ask: Are citizens' hard earned tax dollars spent wisely to meet their needs and within our existing tax revenues? What are the cost effectiveness of each of our programs? What is our strategy for providing a healthy climate for growth, jobs and economic development?

Unfortunately, after all the months of special sessions and debate, the final budget balancing plan adopted by the legislature consisted of a measly $47 million in spending cuts, authorizing the borrowing of up to $150 million against future revenues from the anticipated national tobacco settlement, and asking voters to approve 5% increase in the income tax rate to 9.5% for three years. I opposed this plan because the spending cuts should have been greater, borrowing against future revenue is unwise as it ties up money that might be needed for other priorities in the future, and because Oregon's income tax was already one of the highest in the country, I knew that the voters would reject the increase when they voted in January 2003 (and I was right).

When all the special sessions were done, the Albany Democrat-Herald ran a favorable editorial about my work. They wrote, "Why this compulsion among some legislators to borrow against the future to bail Oregon out of its budget crunch? Why not do what prudent people would do? Senator Mae Yih has been on the Legislature's budget committee for many years, always arguing for living within our means, never promoting tax increases. Now she has proposed an approach that has the mark of common sense...She would cut programs that don't work. She would start with OECDD...She would impose austerity measures on the rest of state government, across-the-board."

In an effort to bring more transparency and public involvement to the state government. I also asked Senate President Derfler if there were any funds available to publish in Oregon's major newspapers the budgets of each government agency, so that citizens could provide input as to: what their high priority and lower priority programs are; what kind of bureaucracy and administrative cuts can be made in the programs to make government more efficient. I also asked for assigning a committee staff to compile the input received by e-mail, fax or letters. I suggested setting up a web-site publishing the list of agency expenditures. People would then be able to respond to the website with their ideas, name, address and telephone number.

The Albany Democrat Herald editorialized "Senator Yih offered the Legislature a plan to get out of its budget mess, a workable plan the majority chose to ignore. Now she has offered another sound idea. She asked the Senate leadership about asking the newspapers in the state to publish budget figures detailed enough to allow the public to make some judgments about spending and cutting back. Yih said this would give the public a chance to express itself on what it regards as high priority items that should be saved at all costs, and which have a lower priority and might, if necessary, be axed. The information is already available on the Internet, but not everyone has access to it. Yih also suggested that the state tally on-line suggestions on what they think should be done about the budget situation. The suggestions might not all be practical, but they might give lawmakers an idea or two, or stiffen their backbones to do one thing or another. Mae Yih has been in the Legislature a long time. Even after all these years, she comes up with ideas that go beyond the usual arguments, but try to involve the people in what the Legislature decides."

With the conclusion of the special sessions, Steve and I were able to travel to China in November to mark my 56th high school reunion and Steve's 80th birthday. We visited his birthplace in Ningpo and his old grade school. Steve was also able to see one of his five brothers in Ningpo. Steve was in seventh heaven, as we were treated to his very favorite dish—raw salted crab. During our travels, however, I noticed that Steve's memory was failing. Once at our hotel and once at the Shanghai airport he wandered off without telling me, and I had to search all over for him. Any last minute regrets I had about retiring from the legislature were eliminated, as I knew that I would need to spend more time with Steve.

Also in November I concluded my 23 years of service as a member of the Linn County Commission on Children and Families (originally titled Commission on Children and Juvenile Services). I had decided that I would end my service on the Commission when I retired from the Legislature. I used my final meeting with the Commission to strongly express my concern with some very disturbing statistics. The statistics were contained in a one-page summary report I had prepared from 35 pages of data that compared Linn County's 1993-2001 benchmark performance with the state average. This way, we can see at a glance whether our investment of time and money over the years was making any improvements. It would help us in allocation of funds in reaching our goals in the priority benchmark programs at a time of limited resources. My summary report revealed that Linn County 8th graders used alcohol, drugs, and tobacco at a higher rate than the state average. Further, Linn County's rate of high school dropouts, juvenile crime arrests and teen pregnancy were also higher than the state average. These numbers were unacceptable, and if the Commission was to turn those numbers around then we had to set priorities, monitor performance outcome, and be accountable for our expenditures. If we wanted to make a difference, then effective prevention was always the best policy. I believed this would also help in slowing the Department of Corrections from building so many prisons, which were a large part of their $835 million budget for the biennium.

My final full month as a legislator was December 2002, and it was memorable for four reasons—one bad, and three good. The bad reason occurred on December 9, when I was driving home from the Oregon Leadership Summit in Portland. I wanted to stop by my office in Salem to pick up some material and somehow got headed in the wrong direction. It was dark in the early evening, and I ended up making a turn at a green traffic light, without waiting for a turn signal, and an oncoming car crashed into the passenger side of my car. The impact caused my head to bump against the ceiling causing a six-inch long cut, and it caused the airbag to inflate, which saved me from more serious injury. I was transported by ambulance to the Salem Hospital where the doctor stitched up my scalp and made sure I hadn't suffered a concussion. Stephen visited me at the hospital and drove me home following a day of observation in the hospital—and he didn't even lecture me about my bad driving habits!

The first good reason that December 2002 was so memorable was that the Taxpayers Association of Oregon made me the only member in the Oregon State Senate to receive the coveted "Taxpayer Watch Dog" Award. In announcing the award, they said "Senator Mae Yih, the Albany Democrat, who is legendary for her singular independence from liberal doctrine and is a determined advocate for reducing the size of government. True to her convictions, Mae surprised many in both parties by courageously advancing a well-constructed plan to eliminate the state's useless and expensive Oregon Economic Development Department. While other lawmakers only gave lip service to solving the state's spending problems, Senator Yih tirelessly worked to produce a variety of budget drafts which did not require any new taxes. In the recent sessions, Mae, under pressure to do otherwise, resolutely stood up for taxpayers by voting no against any new taxes." By the same token, earlier in October, the National Federation of Independent Businesses (NFIB) rated me as having a NFIB voting record of 100% due to my yes votes on a real estate transfer tax moratorium, returning the kicker money to taxpayers, and the implementation of Ballot Measure 50 property tax reduction. They appreciated my no votes on the increases of the gas tax, vehicle registration tax, weight-mile tax, cigarette tax, and income tax.

The second good reason why I fondly remember December 2002 is that I hosted a retirement party and holiday open house at my home in Albany. I invited many friends from Albany and Salem, and was delighted that so many attended, including Senate President Gene Derfler. A reporter from the Albany Democrat Herald also attended, and in the story that was published about the open house, Senator Derfler was quoted as saying that "Mae never quits. Most of the people go 95% of the way and they quit. Mae goes 100%." The story also quoted a guest named Dusty Samard, a labor union lobbyist who worked with me since my first election to the legislature, who said that he would never forget how I had fought to increase wages and death benefits for workers who were injured or killed, an issue that hadn't been addressed for twenty years. And Dusty's wife, Eileen, the mayor of Tangent, was quoted as saying "One of the things I think people are going to miss about Mae is her willingness to talk to anybody. If they had a cause and she agreed with them, she goes to bat for them. It wasn't just lip service. She really did go to work for them."

At the end of the party I told Senator Derfler that I planned to spend my retirement being "fat and sassy." To the laughter of all those gathered around us, he replied by saying "You are already sassy!"

And the third good reason why my last month as a legislator was memorable was that I proved Senator Derfler right—I was sassy and standing up for what I believed. On December 22, the Oregonian, the Eugene Register Guard, the Albany Democrat Herald, the Corvallis Gazette Times and the Sweet Home New Era all published a guest column of mine entitled "Tax hike won't solve problems," that was more or less my farewell statement as a state legislator. The guest column summarized many of the principles and priorities that were the hallmarks of my 26 years in Salem and

13 years on local school boards. Here are some highlights of what I wrote:

"For the first time in 26 years, I will be a private citizen when the Oregon Legislature convenes in January. I would like to offer my observations and advice to those who will now address the state's problems. First, raising taxes will not solve the budget problem. We have come to rely on an unsustainable growth trend in tax revenues. There is little concern for setting priorities or improving efficiency. These issues must be addressed before asking taxpayers for more money....

Neither the outgoing Governor nor the legislature has shown leadership in setting priorities for government spending and for improving efficiency. Many of my colleagues seem more concerned with protecting the dollar amount going to their favored programs than with seeing the money is spent effectively for the people of Oregon. Over the past year, I made a number of recommendations for setting priorities and improving efficiency and have been very disappointed at their reception. Agencies respond to proposed budget cuts by targeting the most visible and useful programs. It is very difficult to cut or eliminate any program, much less make changes that improve efficiency: but this must be the first step.

I have become convinced that our expenditures on economic development are largely wasted. While there are many supporters who received money from the OECDD, it has not prevented the state from leading the nation in unemployment, nor has it resulted in raising Oregon's average income. The department reports great achievements, but an audit by the Secretary of State's office found that the Department's claims of jobs created were only verified in three of nineteen cases where data was available. Fewer jobs or none at all were created in the other sixteen cases. Yet when I tried to get the department's funding reduced so as to redirect it to more compelling needs, I received little support from my colleagues or the Governor.

When the Department of Health and Human Services was instructed to cut its budget, it focused on programs that would generate political outcry rather than low priority areas where savings could be generated. For example, the state operated group homes for the developmentally disabled population has a budget of $77 million for the 2001-03 biennium to serve 156 clients with 726 full time employees. This is a staff to client ration of 4.65-1 at a cost of $246,794 per person per year. If private contractors operated this, the cost could be reduced to less than $125,000 per person per year. The savings can be substantial, but I cannot get support and cooperation of the agency, nor a majority of my colleagues...yet our responsibility is to represent the taxpayers. I also proposed elimination of the Oregon Criminal Justice Commission, whose purpose is to improve the effectiveness and efficiency of the state and local criminal justice systems. In view of the scheduled closures of the four regional juvenile detention centers, selected adult prisons, release of 4,000 inmates, and the layoff of 131 police officers, I believe our priority ought to be to use the $19.2 million commission funding to stabilize our *criminal justice system first before any recommendations of improvement and policy development are made.*

My primary objective is to voice my observation that state agencies are cutting essential services in their budget adjustments when they need to prioritize and eliminate low priority, non-essential services, duplications, bureaucracy and red tape, and implement cost savings and efficiency measures. We do this at home and in our businesses when revenue declines; why don't we apply the same logic in government? We need to evaluate the cost effectiveness of each state agency and, where possible, evaluate the state's return on investment. If we take out the wants, preserved the needs, and live within our income, we will go a long way in regaining the public's trust in government. If we can make our agencies efficient and keep our taxes low, our economy will recover and prosper sooner. It will take hard work, but Oregon citizens deserve no less, and will benefit greatly in the short and long term."

My guest column drew nine letters to the editor from citizens in Lebanon, Portland, Tangent, Albany, Brownsville and Corvallis. Seven of these nine were very supportive of my position and two were opposed.

Another letter to the editor has a special place in my heart. It appeared in the Albany Democrat Herald on November 23, 2002, a few weeks after Frank Morse was elected to replace me in the Oregon State Senate. Jean and Kevin Burger of Cascadia wrote, *"Mae, we're going to miss you! It's kind of like having that feisty watchdog we've always counted on being taken away and being replaced by something in the back of the dog house and we're really not sure what it is. But then again, Mae Yih spoiled us. She is definitely feisty and always ready to go to bat for her constituents. She saved the bridge in Cascadia, found federal funding and changed a few minds. She took on a state agency and helped it to do what it was meant to do, just to name a few things that this incredible lady did. She always put her constituents first, and worked some long hours to do that and while we are willing to give the "new kids" the benefit of the doubt, they've got some pretty big shoes to fill, and so they'd better eat their Wheaties. We'll miss you Mae."*

CHAPTER 6: **Life After the Legislature**

When the 2003 session of the Oregon State Legislature convened at the State Capitol on January 13, I have to confess that it felt very strange not to be there. After all, I had been on the floor of the State House of Representatives or State Senate for every regular and special session since January 1977. It was a rewarding and challenging 26 years, and I worked as hard as I could until almost the very last minute.

On January 10, just three days before my final Senate term expired, I attended my last meeting of the Joint Legislative Emergency Board. I did so also to complete an action that I had requested and had been previously approved by the Legislative Ways and Means Committee during the 2001 session. The request was that a review be made of the cost of the services that the Department of Human Services was providing to medically fragile individuals with developmental disabilities. The Emergency Board approved that an oversight committee be appointed to complete the review, but when one was not appointed, it was agreed that I could serve as a one-member oversight committee.

I requested this report because I was very concerned that in a time of a severe budget crisis, with Oregon facing a $2 billion shortfall that might require cuts in programs that help frail and disabled seniors, DHS was ignoring efficiency measures that could result in significant savings. The information I gathered in preparing my report more than supported my concerns.

For example, I received information that it cost $112,114 per month to care for three individuals in a state operated medical group home. These costs included a staff of 21—a staff to client ratio of 7 to 1— but did not include the cost of special food and pharmaceuticals. One of the three clients required special food imported from Europe, as well as two medications that cost $6,000 to $7,000 per drug per month. The same group home was billing the state $3,000 a month for a full-time manual arts instructor who planned programs for the three clients—one who went to school full-time and two who worked part-time. Compare this one planner for three clients ratio to a medical group home operated by the private sector, where one social worker planned for 30 clients! The state operated medical homes were also regularly providing 25 hours a week in enhanced services such as excursions to the Columbia River Gorge on a sternwheeler and to the Oregon beaches. When I asked why they were providing these enhanced programs when the state was cutting basic and essential services, I was told it was a federal requirement. I knew, however, that the state was operating under a federal waiver and that it was inconceivable that the state did not ask for an exemption during a time of budgetary constraint so that savings could be used to preserve higher priority programs.

Other information I received in preparing the report revealed that state operated group homes paid $14 a pill for a certain medicine, when the market price was only $4 a pill. State operated homes were also contracting occupational therapists and physical therapists at $100 per hour, when private sector providers were contracting these services at half the cost.

As reported by the DHS, the cost per client in the state operated medical group homes averaged $19,000 a month. Community medical group homes were providing care at a range of $8,900 to $12,500 per client per month. DHS claimed that part of this cost difference was due to the fact that state operated homes were caring for clients of a much higher acuity level, but they were unwilling to release care plans without patient names that supported their argument, nor were they willing to allow visits to these group homes. I couldn't help but question their reasoning that only state operated group homes were capable of providing for clients of high acuity levels. According to the University of the Minnesota study entitled "Residential Services for Persons with Developmental Disabilities: Status and Trends Through 2000," Oregon's daily average rate for care in state MRDD facilities was the second highest in the nation. This study reported the national average as $296.22 per day for homes with 1 to 6 residents. Oregon's cost was $582.26 per day—second only to New Hampshire, and almost twice the national average.

The bottom line was that Oregon was in a huge budget crisis and we were facing a $2 billion revenue shortfall in the coming biennium. We were cutting mental health programs, alcohol and chemical dependency treatment programs, and nursing home rates, which would likely cause the closure of nursing homes, displacing many frail and disabled seniors. Given all this, I simply didn't understand why DHS wasn't proposing efficiency measures in programs where there could be significant savings. These potential savings could then be used for preserving many of our high priority programs from deeper cuts.

At the conclusion of the meeting, I recommended that the DHS director review the high staffing levels and costs of the state operated group homes and compare those with the private community group home rates and costs of other states' programs, and, as soon as possible, propose to the next legislature and Governor how adequate services and supplies could be provided more efficiently and at less cost.

When the meeting adjourned—my last meeting as a member of the Oregon State Legislature—I took pride in the fact that I did my job and represented my constituents to the best of my abilities to the very last minute, and that I had steadfastly fulfilled the commitment I made starting in my 1975 school board campaign of achieving maximum results with minimum of cost for my constituents, community and state.

I didn't decide to run for the school board or the legislature to receive recognition, but it certainly is rewarding when your hard work and efforts are recognized. I was very proud in March 2003, when the Albany Chamber of Commerce presented me with their Distinguished Service Award—similar to the First Citizen award that Steve had received 34 years earlier. In presenting the award to me, Ron Loney, the Director of the Albany Boys and Girls Club said that I was a "shining example to the rest of us, and we are fortunate to have her in our community." He also said that I was "extraordinarily persistent, has an untiring approach, and never gives up." I used my acceptance remarks to explain that I was the one who should be offering thanks for all the community of Albany had done to help me and my family over the years. I also said that it was "only in America where I could receive such an honor."

One of the main reasons I decided to retire from the legislature was to spend more time with Steve and 2003 provided plenty of opportunity for doing just that.

We celebrated our 50th wedding anniversary in June by traveling to the Oregon coast for a weekend, and then we flew to Chicago for a week with our entire family.

You might remember that during this trip your grandfather told the story of how his great grandfather Ye Cheng Zhong's honesty was key to him starting his business. He had a sampan boat rowing business. One day, he waited to return a businessman's attaché case that had been left behind in his boat. The case contained important documents and a large sum of money. The businessman was so impressed by great grandfather's honesty that he introduced him to important contacts that helped him start his import and export business. After achieving considerable success, great grandfather established a tuition-free primary and high school in Shanghai for low-income students so that children like him could receive a good education. I share that story because Steve and I would visit that school in October 2003 as we made a trip to China as part of our 50th wedding anniversary celebration.

Retirement from the legislature did allow me the time to take care of some "downsizing" actions. First, I helped Steve sell one of his investments—a 40-unit apartment building in Salem. The manager of the apartment building was neglecting his duties and not collecting rent in a timely fashion nor keeping up the maintenance of the building. Steve's deteriorating health prohibited him from taking over the management, and selling it was the right step to take. I also was able to sell Steve's 1977 Silver Shadow II Rolls Royce. The car had sat in the garage for several years without much use, except when a friend wanted to borrow it for a wedding or special occasion. The Rolls Royce had gained a little bit of fame years earlier when I drove it to the Capitol on a day when my car didn't work, and parked it in my assigned parking spot. Ron Blankenbaker, the long-time political columnist for the Salem Statesman-Journal saw it there, where I had parked next to a Volkswagen owned by a Republican legislator. Blankenbaker challenged his readers to guess which car belonged to a Democrat and which belonged to a Republican. Of course, everyone guessed the Rolls belonged to a Republican and the Volkswagen belonged to a Democrat!

When I retired from the Legislature, I looked forward to many years of relaxation, togetherness and traveling with your grandfather. 2003 was a fun and memorable year, as we made the trips to China and Chicago I described in the previous chapter. Unfortunately, they were the last vacations that Steve and I would take together. Retirement quickly became an unforeseen nightmare.

The fact is that from April of 2004 through March of 2009 my days and nights were devoted entirely to caring for Steve as he battled one medical crisis after another. These were without a doubt the most difficult, most exhausting and loneliest times of my life. There were days and nights when I was so stressed and exhausted that I believed I could not go on one minute more. I wished almost every day that my sons Donald or Daniel could drop everything and come home to help me handle all the responsibilities. In my heart, however, I realized that was not practical. I tried to remember the old Chinese saying that "Contentment is happiness." I knew that I should feel content that Steve and I had provided our sons with the best care and education, and they had used that education to build successful careers and families in the east coast—Donald, a cardiologist in Philadelphia, and Daniel a former attorney and current business executive in Connecticut, far away from Oregon. I should also feel content that Steve had made a good living, that we had enough to live on during retirement and that we had good health insurance to cover Steve's medical issues. No matter how tired I was, I got up every morning knowing that I was where I needed to be, and that my duty was to do everything I could to help my husband—a husband who was brilliant, thoughtful, kind, generous, hard-working and compassionate toward his family, colleagues, and community. Steve showed great courage and perseverance in dealing with an endless series of medical problems that would have caused most individuals to just give up.

Steve's medical issues had begun earlier, with prostate cancer diagnosed in 1987 and treated with radiation. In 1997 he had a stroke due to blood clots from his heart because of an irregular heart beat called atrial flutter. This was treated with a blood thinner. He then developed Type II Diabetes in 2000. Despite having diabetes, he was simply unable to control his passion for eating strawberry pancakes with whipped cream for breakfast. The inappropriate diet meant that his blood sugars were not properly controlled.

The permanent medical deterioration began in April 2004, when he tripped and fell by the step to our garage. I was in the kitchen, and heard his call for help. I was unable to lift him, and had to call 911 to have paramedics come out. They realized he had broken his hip and took him to the hospital. Donald came home and consulted with a local orthopedic doctor. They decided to pin the broken bones, and Steve returned home after three days in the hospital.

Unfortunately, the pinning of the broken bones was not successful. Steve was soon experiencing a great deal of pain, and in August 2004 it was recommended that he undergo a total replacement of his right hip. Steve remained in the hospital for three days following the surgery, and was then sent by the surgeon to a care facility in Albany for ten days of recuperation and physical therapy. Steve was reluctant to do the exercises prescribed by the physical therapist, and he soon was diagnosed with a blood clot. The clot treatment would eventually lead to internal bleeding that required Steve to receive a blood transfusion. Steve's condition was further aggravated when the incision from his hip surgery would not heal correctly. As a result, between September 5 and September 29, I would call 911 seven times, and rush Steve to the hospital emergency room six times, where he would be examined by seventeen different doctors.

More bad news was to come as Steve developed chronic drainage from his hip wound, which would lead to unsuccessful plastic surgery; procedures to allow the use of a vacuum pump to close the wound; development of pneumonia that brought a persistent and severe form of diarrhea; occasional black-outs and loss of consciousness due to elevated levels of potassium; and one occasion where his heart was at risk of stopping, requiring him to be air lifted to Portland.

Perhaps one day stands as the clearest example of the challenges I faced. It was September 6, 2004. The night before Steve had made an emergency trip from the care facility to the hospital to check on a high temperature and a dark red hip wound. The hospital then sent him back to the care facility. After dashing between the hospital and the care facility, I had arrived home well after midnight. I received a call about 8:30 a.m. the next morning to tell me that Steve had a seizure rendering him speechless, and was being sent to the hospital emergency room again. With barely little sleep, I hurried to the hospital. On the drive over, I didn't see a stop sign and ran into another car. The accident resulted in one severely cracked tooth which was quite painful and would require dental work later on, but, thankfully, the other driver was not injured. My car was damaged, and the police officer who responded to the accident drove me to the hospital. The emergency room doctor told me that Steve was having internal bleeding, and would need a blood transfusion. I remained at the hospital until the blood transfusion was successfully completed at 5:30p.m. While there, I had to make a series of phone calls— one to my insurance agent to report the accident and to reinstate insurance on Steve's car so I could use it while mine was being repaired; one to the towing company to take my car from the site of the accident to the repair shop; one to my dentist to make an appointment to fix my cracked tooth; and one to a friend who gave me a ride to the care facility so I could pick up Steve's clothes, walker and leg brace before I returned home. After I arrived home, I tried to start Steve's car, which had not been driven for several months, so I could go buy something to eat, and found that it was completely dead. I called AAA, who came out and jumped the battery. After driving to and from the grocery store, I finally got to bed at 11:30p.m. What a day!

There were other similarly hectic and stressful days that followed, as Steve's hip wound would require special care for the rest of his life—as would his diabetes, which would eventually lead to years of kidney dialysis. My daily schedule for nearly five years included giving Steve insulin shots, even though I dreaded the sight of poking a needle into someone's body; cleaning Steve's hip wound meticulously and changing the dressing on his wound two or three times each day; (a process that required using a long stem Q tip to insert a ribbon of sterile gauze into the wound to allow proper draining, resulting in two occasions when the Q-tip fractured inside the wound, forcing me to call 911 to take Steve to the emergency room so they could be removed), putting tight orthopedic stockings on Steve's legs in order to improve his circulation; and getting Steve and his wheelchair in the car and driving him to his three times a week dialysis appointments. Steve's restricted diet meant low fat, low salt, low sugar, low potassium, low starch and limited fluids. For someone who had no medical knowledge or training, it was a very harrowing learning experience to correctly and instantly perform each task.

Thankfully, I was assisted during much of Steve's illnesses by a number of caregivers and physical therapists who came to our home, as well as a dietician and a retired Chinese chef who helped with Steve's very restricted diet. Without all of them, I wouldn't have been able to get any sleep or complete the 24/7 responsibilities of caring for Steve. (I especially remember the caregiver who called home every lunch break to talk to her pet bird who refused to eat when she was absent. Her grandmother would answer the phone, and hold it up so the bird could hear her voice, and she would tell it to eat!)

I wish I could have hired somebody to help me with a chore I undertook in 2008. While Steve was at his 2.5-hour long dialysis appointments three times a week, I would drive home to clean up our barn, garage, and basement. I had concluded that it would be wise for Steve and me to downsize and move into a senior community or a smaller home closer to the hospital. In addition to cleaning up 43 years of "junk" that had accumulated since we built the house, I also had to clean the barn, which included two-inch thick layers of old horse manure, as well as old straw and oats, countless spider webs, and dead mice. It was the dirtiest job of my whole life!

In February 2009, it became clear that Steve was in his final weeks. He was so weak and immobile that he required a lifting machine to move him from his bed to his wheelchair and for all other movements during the day. His kidney doctor recommended that we should stop dialysis as the treatment was no longer helping him. Don and Dan came home and on March 7, Steve consented to having his dialysis treatment stopped. Six days later, on March 13, 2009, my husband of nearly 56 years passed away. I knew that after years of enduring so much pain that he was in a better place, but I was still so very sad. There was a beautiful funeral service on March 19, where Donald and Daniel gave very touching and heartwarming eulogies for their father, and the grandsons who always filled him with so much pride read Biblical scriptures.

In the weeks and months following Steve's passing, I gave a great deal of thought to the best way to honor his life and legacy. I eventually decided that the most fitting way was to pay tribute to the key pioneering role that Steve played in making Albany and the surrounding area the refractory metal capital of the United States and one of the outstanding centers in the world.

Due to Steve's foresight of the need for finished zirconium products, he took calculated risks in investing in multi-million dollar rolling and fabrication plants, thereby becoming the nation's only completely integrated producer of reactor-grade zirconium mill products from ore to finished product. Steve first started construction of the plant in 1956 and delivered zirconium in four months—one month ahead of the deadline given him by the U.S. Atomic Energy Commission and the U.S. Navy. Steve lived in his boots during a typical cold wet Oregon winter as he went on a 24-hour non-stop work schedule to get it done.

Employment at Wah Chang increased from 80 in 1956 to over 1,400 in 1975, when Steve resigned. By 2015, Linn County's primary metals sector employed over 2,000 people. These were high-paying jobs, with an annual average wage over $68,000—96% higher than the average wage for all industries in Linn County. The jobs and the salaries were critical to a local economy that had long depended on the agriculture and timber industries, which were very seasonal. It is important to note that the vast majority of the revenue produced by Wah Chang and the county's metal companies is from customers outside of the local economy. These customers inject money into the local economy through corporate and property taxes, employee wages, and local spending. Jobs in the primary metals industry have a significant multiplier effect on the local economy. It is estimated that for every new job created in Linn County's primary metals sector, an additional 1.15 jobs are created in the community. Linn County's primary metal manufacturing sector paid over $1.6 million in property taxes in 2007-2008, and the properties have an estimated real market value of over $123 million.

Steve resigned in 1975 due to a disagreement in management policy with Teledyne, the Los Angeles based parent conglomerate company. Steve was under constant pressure to increase prices, despite long-term contracts with customers that locked in stable pricing. Steve would not violate his integrity and principle of doing business. When Teledyne transferred him to Far East Asian operations, he resigned. When he left, his colleagues presented him with a specialty metals collection, which included zirconium, hafnium, titanium, niobium, tantalum and tungsten. I had that collection installed in a custom designed showcase and in September 2009, I donated the showcase—entitled "Contributions to Reactive and Refractory Metals: A History of Special Metals in Albany" to West Albany High School. I worked with Ron Graham, the retired vice president and technology director of ATI Wah Chang to ensure the showcase explained the production and uses of each of the metals. The display is a tribute to Stephen's pioneer achievements in the metals industry. These metals can withstand extreme environments, including high temperatures and exposure to strong acids and chemicals. This metal capital came into existence as a direct result of the strong effort of local citizens and the global needs for high performance metals.

The display was intended to help students understand the local metal industries, the importance of and demand for the metals, and to inspire students to study science and math so they can expand their career paths and make contributions that would improve the quality of life. Students could see from the showcase that products made from metals produced at ATI Wah Chang were used for the military, naval defense, nuclear energy electricity generating plants, aerospace, transportation, medical applications, superconductivity, fiber-optic applications, research and more. From stents placed in a human heart to orthopedic implants that lasted ten times longer than previous ones to rocket nozzles that helped transport mankind into the far expanses of outer space, metals produced at ATI Wah Chang made a daily difference in people's lives.

I also hoped that the display and Steve's story would remind students that America is a land of freedom and opportunities and serve as an example of how an individual from humble beginnings could achieve great accomplishments through a good education, hard work, determination, high integrity and compassion for his or her community and fellow citizens.

As another tribute to Steve, I donated $15,000 to the Colorado School of Mines, in honor of Charles Baroch, who served as a mentor to Steve during his time as a titanium researcher at the Bureau of Mines in Boulder City, Nevada, and $10,000 to each Albany high school to support their math and science departments. Donald, Daniel, and I also established an endowment fund which distributed $5,000 for an annual college scholarship for a needy student with good academic performance who is entering into the math, science or engineering fields. This scholarship was in special memory of the extreme financial hardship Steve endured during his graduate studies when he first came to America. He arrived with only $500 in his pocket, and he struggled with various summer and part-time jobs to meet graduate school tuition and living expenses. During this time, he would eat pancakes for three meals a day, and sometimes when he was short of money he would walk over 100 blocks from his graduate school, Brooklyn Polytechnical Institute, to his uptown basement apartment. With his height of 5'10", he weighed only 120 pounds!

In addition to the annual scholarship, since 2009, I have also sponsored a "Renaissance in Science" essay contest for students at the two high schools in Albany. The contest encourages students to think critically as they research and address issues relating to the environment, space exploration, and physics. The author of the first prize essay receives $1,200, and the author of the second prize essay receives $800. I also award $500 to the science teachers who mentor the essay participants at each school. The judges for the initial contest were representatives from ATI Wah Chang, Linn-Benton Community College, and the U.S. Department of Energy's National Energy Technology Laboratory in Albany. The top winning essays were then sent to state and federal officials for their review and comment, including the United States Secretary of Energy, Steven Chu. Secretary Chu responded with a gracious letter stating that "stimulating interest in math and science is critical to our nation's future." Secretary Chu also sent the winning essays to three of the Department of Energy's Albert Einstein Distinguished Educator Fellows for review, and they provided thoughtful comments and encouragement for the essay winners to apply for undergraduate internships at the DOE Pacific Northwest National Laboratory.

I continued to sponsor this contest, and highlight a different topic every year. Topics have included energy independence; the history and uses of specialty metals, including niobium, titanium and others. Niobium is a metal used in MRI machines, maglev trains, and the large Hadron Collider, a proton beam accelerator in Switzerland, which allows scientists to detect the Higgs Boson—the elementary particle that contains all of an atom's mass. It uses superconducting magnets and cable made from niobium-titanium alloy, which is mainly produced at ATI Wah Chang in Albany,

I am pleased to report that the winning essays have remained very impressive every year since the contest began. I especially want to mention the winning essays by West Albany High School students Ashleigh Pilkerton in 2010 and Rachel Proteau in 2013. Ashleigh's essay focused on the use of buoys to harness wave energy. She received strong encouragement from the Department of Energy to apply for an undergraduate internship at the Department's Pacific Northwest National Laboratory, located in the State of Washington. Rachel's essay focused on the history and uses of niobium. She was invited to tour ATI Wah Chang and learn more about niobium and the process they use to manufacture it and its alloys. At the request of the Albany high school science teachers, in 2014 I replaced the science essay contest with two summer science internships at Oregon State University which were part of a "Saturday Academy" program sponsored by the University of Portland. The essay contest returned in 2016.

In the years following Steve's passing, I also devoted a great deal of time and energy to writing his biography. It was a project I began when I retired from the legislature in 2003. I had hoped that Steve would be able to provide me by sharing stories from his life and career, but his health complications would have a detrimental impact on his memory. I then turned to newspaper clippings that I had collected over the years, and I also interviewed many of Steve's longtime colleagues and friends.

I finished the biography in 2011 and gave the 55 printed copies to family, friends, businesses in the metals industry, and local schools, universities, and community libraries. The biography was written in memory of the hardship Steve endured in paying for his graduate school tuition and living expenses, the pioneering work he did in the metals industry, and the qualities he exhibited throughout his life—hard work, determination, high integrity, love and compassion for his family, colleagues and community. The book was intended to serve as an inspiration to our grandchildren and students of how an individual from humble beginnings can achieve great accomplishments in America, a land of freedom and opportunities.

Steve's biography was dedicated to his great grandfather, Ye Cheng Zhong, whose high integrity and hard work led him to rise from a humble beginning as a sampan ferry rowboat man to become the owner of a successful enterprise of import and export of metals and kerosene, as well as a real estate business that included large holdings of commercial properties in Shanghai. I also dedicated it to all the generations of Steve's family, past and present, whose dreams, sorrows and steadfastness led and guided him, to his colleagues and employees who supported his efforts and innovations in the building and diversification of Wah Chang, and to the communities of Albany and Millersburg, especially during the beginning years when government contracts were short and finance was lean. Finally, the biography was written also to honor Mr. K.C. Li, Sr., Chairman of the Board of Directors of Wah Chang Corporation in New York, whose inspiration and trust helped Steve in seeking what Mr. Li termed "the eagles in the productive sky—Hafnium, Zirconium, Titanium, Tantalum, Columbium, Molybdenum, and Tungsten—exotic metals of the atomic age, which are proclaiming the dawn of a new industrial era."

In 2012 and 2013, I was assisted by Oregon State University graduates Mao Mei Yue and her husband, Wei Ming Dai, in translating Steve's biography into Chinese. Mao Mei Yue was one of five students from Fujian province and Shanghai whom I sponsored each for two years of graduate studies at Oregon State University since 1986. My goal in translating Steve's biography into Chinese was to give a copy of the translated biography to the Ye Cheng Zhong primary and high schools that Steve's great grandfather had founded in Shanghai. This school was tuition-free for low income students so that children like him could receive a good education. The Ye Cheng Zhong School still operates today and takes up almost a whole block in the Hongkou district of Shanghai. In 2015, I traveled to Shanghai to participate in the 115th anniversary of the school. I was proud to present the translated Stephen Yih biography "The Life and Career of a Metals Pioneer Stephen Wei-Hong Yih," and an annual Stephen Yih memorial college scholarship in the amount of $5,000 to the school to encourage the study of science and technology and to assist needy students in the pursuit of higher education.

As I write this book, it has been over seven years since Steve's passing. I still miss him every day, and still marvel at his accomplishments and his remarkable life. I hope that you will always remember him and how much he loved you.

During his declining health, Steve insisted that even though he couldn't travel with me, I needed to take a break from the stress and pressure and enjoy family vacations. During these times, I arranged for home health care workers to provide full time care service.

These trips included a 2004 trip to Italy and London with Daniel, Nancy, Stephen, Christopher and Benjamin. When Daniel and Nancy took some time to cruise the Mediterranean with friends, I got the opportunity to "babysit." We had a wonderful time visiting historic sites, riding gondolas in Venice, and eating lots of spaghetti and gelato. Above all, it was a wonderful opportunity to bond with my grandsons. They especially enjoyed my stories about their father and uncle as young boys.

In 2005, I met my sons and their families in New York City, and we took in the United States Open tennis championship. Tennis has long been our "family sport," as

Steve played when he was growing up in Shanghai, and both Donald and Daniel played in school. And instead of just watching while Donald and Daniel took tennis lessons, I took them, too! I believe having played tennis every day before being elected to the legislature gave me good foot work and stamina for campaigning door-to-door. A special family tradition was that Donald and Daniel would play doubles tennis with me and Steve on my birthday—and their present to me was that they would let us win!

In 2007, Dan and Nancy invited me to join them for a 10-day vacation in Cambodia, Thailand, Laos and Myanmar. We visited many ancient temples and palaces, and stayed in an elephant sanctuary in Thailand. The highlight of the trip was crossing a pond while riding on elephants and having the elephants decided to bathe themselves! It was hilarious and we all got very wet.

My 2008 break was a trip to China with my brother, Jim, to celebrate my 80th birthday. Jim had recently retired as Senior Director of Corporate Research for Anheuser-Busch Company in St. Louis, Missouri. Jim received his Ph.D. in chemistry while working full-time and raising a family—showing the same determination our father had shown when he studied the English dictionary at midnight by candlelight as a young overworked apprentice. While in Shanghai, we visited with our two half-brothers and two half-sisters, their spouses, and my old high school classmates. About twelve of us traveled by minibus 150 miles west of Shanghai where we visited my father's birthplace, and the Jiang Ying Native Son Institute, where my father was prominently listed with his portrait and biography as an industrialist giant. Brother Jim and I also rode the Maglev train on our way back to the Shanghai airport. This magnetic levitation train is the fastest in the world and has no wheels, no engine, no tracks, and is completely noiseless. The Maglev train uses a niobium-titanium alloy to power superconducting levitation magnets. Back in the 1960's, at least 2000 feet of niobium wire was needed to wind around test magnets. At the time, no company in the world could make niobium wire that long without it breaking. It was Wah Chang, under Steve's dedication and leadership, who devised a procedure to make niobium wires of longer lengths. That breakthrough process was reported by the New York Times on August 13, 1961.

Family trips have continued since Steve's passing, and in December 2009, I visited Donald, Pam and Alex in Philadelphia and then went to visit Daniel, Nancy and grandsons and we flew to Rome on Christmas Day. We visited Rome, Florence, Pompeii, Naples and the Vatican. I was especially impressed with Pompeii, which was built in 500 BC, destroyed by a volcano eruption in 100 AD, and the ruins were discovered in the 1800's. While in Naples, we enjoyed excellent pizza, with a thin crust that was baked with special fruit wood fuel. The tours of the Vatican and St. Peter's Cathedral were extremely impressive. We traveled back to Connecticut on January 1, and finally returned to Oregon on January 3.

2010 was a busy travel year as my trips included attending grandson Stephen's graduation from Thatcher School in Ojai, California, visiting my brother Jim and his wife Beverly in Missouri, attending grandson Alex's graduation from Friends Central School in Philadelphia (where he graduated with high honors and served as student body president), having a wonderful reunion with my Barnard College friend Helen Cheng and her husband in Myrtle Beach, South Carolina, attending the Committee of 100 meeting in San Francisco, and traveling to China with Donald and Pam.

The trip to China was especially memorable as we were met at the airport by Wang Xiao Yen, who was a Shanghai Bureau of Environmental Protection official I sponsored in 2000 for graduate studies in Portland State University for environmental and land use subjects. She was one of five Chinese students I sponsored since1986 to attend two years of graduate studies each in Oregon universities in the areas of agriculture, forestry, environmental science and land use planning. Wang had gone on to become section chief of land use planning in the Bureau. Not only did she pick us up at the airport in her own car, she also arranged for special dinners, and VIP treatment at the Shanghai World Expo, where we didn't have to wait in long lines, and were shuttled from pavilion to pavilion by golf cart. Most importantly, she remains in close contact with her professors at Portland State University, ensuring continued research and joint projects between Shanghai and Oregon. The theme of the Expo was "Better City, Better Future," and included a focus on conservation, recycling, and technological innovation. The shuttle buses were electric, and the water supply was from rain reservoirs. While in Shanghai, we also visited the Palace Hotel, a 200 room hotel located in the Bund, the premier business and international trade district. The hotel was owned by my father from 1947 to 1949 and "joint ventured" with the Chinese government until 1956 when he "contributed" it to the government and received certain "dividends" for his contribution. It was eventually renamed the Peace Hotel and is revered as a symbol of Shanghai's glory days when the city was known as the "Pearl of the Orient."

Another memorable trip to China occurred in 2012, when I made a 19-day tour of Shandong province, three other northeastern provinces, and Shanghai. The highlights of the trip included climbing Mt. Taishan, visiting the Confucius residence and temple, and a visit to a tiger reserve park in Harbin which featured approximately 1,200 tigers, several ligers (off spring of a male lion and female tiger), and white tigers. I also enjoyed a wonderful reunion with four half-brothers and sisters, and high school classmates I went to school with 66 years ago.

The trips that have meant the most to me in recent years are the trips that Donald and Daniel make to Albany for visits, and the trip that I have made to help celebrate the educational milestones of my wonderful grandsons. I especially remember Dan's visit to Oregon in May of 2013 to help celebrate my 85th birthday, and Don's visit that September. Dan and I had a great time visiting some of the covered bridges that I had helped to preserve during my service in the State Senate, and Don and I had a very successful day fishing on the McKenzie River. The fish were biting right and left, and I can still taste the delicious fried trout lunch that was the result of the morning's catch!

My holiday tradition the past few years has been to travel to the east coast, where my family has spoiled me by taking me to Broadway plays, the Rockefeller Center Christmas show, and shopping on New York City's famed 5th Avenue.

My December 2014 visit back east also included witnessing grandson Alex graduate magna cum laude from Brown University in Providence, Rhode Island. I couldn't help but be pleasantly surprised when the university president told the graduates that they needed to use their education to carry out their social responsibility—the very same message that Barnard College President Millicent McIntosh delivered to my classmates and me some sixty-three years before!

Attending Alex's graduation also reminded me of how proud Steve and I were to attend Donald's graduation from medical school and Daniel's graduation from law school. I also thought back to the fact that after Donald's first year in medical school he decided he wanted to continue his summer job in San Francisco as a warehouse worker making $20 an hour. When Donald told him this news, Steve got so mad that he threw his coffee mug against the wall. I happened to pick up the broken cup and placed it in a cabinet. At the end of the summer, Seve flew to San Francisco and brought Donald home. Donald did return to medical school. After his graduation, Steve took the broken cup to Hong Kong where it was glued back together with a gold frame and handle. The cup now sits in Donald's living room as a great memento.

Other recent family gatherings included grandson Benjamin's June 2015 graduation from Thatcher School—a boarding school in Ojai, California, and grandson Stephen's June 2015 graduation with honors from Northwestern University in Evanston, Illinois. Benjamin went on to a "gap year" touring Indonesia with a student group before joining his brother, Christopher, at Dartmouth in the fall of 2016. Stephen is now working at an investment firm in Los Angeles.

Retiring from the legislature didn't mean that I stopped having opinions on the issues of the day. I have continued to carefully read the Albany newspaper each day, and was surprised and delighted and flattered in 2011 to read a letter to the editor that was titled "We Miss Mae Yih." The writer of the letter explained that the current elected state legislators were not providing the same kind of constituent service that I had provided. The letter said, "As we head into this community-wide issue and our attempts to share this and our concerns with our elected representatives, we realized just how spoiled we as constituents were by former State Senator Mae Yih. Mae was there 365 days a year and you could call 24/7 and she would get back to you in person." It was gratifying to know that people still remembered my public service eight years after I had left office.

And it was while reading the local newspaper on October 1, 2012, that I happened to notice a letter to the editor announcing an essay contest with a $2,000 prize. The topic of the contest was "Leading and Uniting America in a Time of Change," and the entrants were instructed to imagine that just like they might be randomly selected for jury duty, they were picked to immediately become President of the United States. The topic of the essay was how they would demonstrate leadership in dealing with the problems facing our country. Entries had to be 1200 words or less and the deadline was January 21, 2013. The contest was targeted at people under the age of 25, but the rules stated that entries would be accepted from anyone who was young enough to look ahead—and that included me! I was challenged by the request to propose solutions to our national problems, and decided to enter the contest. I started re-reading the book "Free to Choose" during a long flight to and from China and was inspired again by the words and ideas of the authors, Nobel Laureate economist Milton Friedman, and his wife, Rose. I had long been an admirer of their advocacy of America's founding principles in liberty and free market, and quoted many of their recommendations in my essay.

I took a great deal of time in writing the essay, and my first draft reached 4,000 words—far over the limit. A Portland State University Economics professor helped me edit the essay down to 1200 words by eliminating many of the examples I used to illustrate my points, and I submitted it by the deadline. I was disappointed when I was informed that even though I had retired from the legislature for nine years, my time there put me in a category as a "professional," rather than the "average citizen" for whom the contest was created. Despite my disqualification, I felt my time in writing and submitting the essay was well spent, as I outlined the steps necessary to tackle our $16 trillion national debt, the ever-growing cost of entitlement programs, expanding government bureaucracies, over-regulation that impedes job opportunities, high taxes, and declining economic growth. My proposals may not have been politically feasible, but they did deserve serious consideration. I was pleased that my proposal regarding Medicare was similar to the plan put forward by Congressman Paul Ryan, 2012 Vice Presidential candidate and current Speaker of the United States House of Representatives. My original essay is included as an attachment at the end of this book, and I hope you will take the time to read it.

※

CHAPTER 7: Letters From The Past

While writing this memoir has taken a great deal of time and work, it has also brought back some wonderful memories—and a very gratifying surprise. The surprise was a package of twenty-six letters from federal, state and community leaders and citizens that had been presented to me in March of 2003 when the Albany Chamber of Commerce honored me with a Distinguished Service Award for my 39 years in public service. I remember them giving me the package of letters, but I can't recall why I never opened and read them at the time.

I found the letters in 2015 as I was reviewing old files for material to include in my book. This time I opened and read them, and was honored and humbled by the kind words about my service. As I reflected on my life, there were times when I wondered whether devoting so much time to public service was worth the time spent away from family. The letters didn't answer that question, but they did give me a sense of satisfaction that my service had made a positive difference for my constituents, my community, and my state. Here are some excerpts from those letters:

Oregon Governor John Kitzhaber wrote, "I think that our friendship pays tribute to the fact that people with often divergent political philosophies can work closely together on areas of common interest. I have the deepest respect for you and for the contributions you have made to this state and to your district."

Senate President Gene Derfler wrote, "Senator Yih is the consummate legislator, representing the best interests of her district with unmatched fervor...Senator Yih's constituents can always count on their legislator to be knowledgeable on many issues and diligently researching for further insight. In the legislative process, she has always asked insightful questions and made important observations to the benefit of all."

Former Senate President Brady Adams wrote, "You have taught me many things. I have watched you fight for the things you believe in when others would throw up their hands and quit. Your actions taught me to have the guts and courage to stand up for what is right...Your dedication to the average person is the model that our forefathers had in mind when they adopted a citizen legislator form of government...I always prided myself on my work ethic, but no matter how early I would get to the Capitol, or how late I would stay, you would be there earlier and stay longer....You read every bill and studied every report. You did your homework. Oregon is a better place because of all that you have done for the state, and I am a better person because of our friendship."

Former Speaker of the House Larry Campbell wrote, "If you have been blessed (a blessing indeed) by being a constituent of Mae's, you were being represented by the best. To say she was persistent in achieving her objectives is an understatement."

United States Senator Ron Wyden wrote, "Mae is the embodiment of the Oregon maverick tradition. As a woman, she forged a trail into politics and became an early leader and role model for a generation of young, centrist, rural women. She has avoided political pigeonholes and proven that a Democrat can be pro-growth, pro-worker, and pro-family. Mae has never been afraid to stand her ground, and in the tradition of Wayne Morse and Tom McCall, she stands as a symbol of the moral imperative that public officials should answer first and foremost to their constituents and their conscience."

Albany City Manager Steve Bryant wrote, "Mae is perhaps the most recognizable figure in Linn County history, and she probably knows more people on a first name basis than anyone else I know. She has dedicated herself to a very high calling and has served the needs of Linn County selflessly…It was always interesting to watch a state official squirm with particular discomfort when Mae would lead an interrogation as to why her constituents weren't receiving the funding or answers they needed to solve a problem…I think it was the tenacity of her purpose that got things done for our community."

Linn County Sheriff David Burright wrote, "Although Mae may be small in stature, she is truly a giant when it comes to will and determination. Her zeal and bulldog are legend in the halls of the Capitol. It was well known that once Senator Yih sunk her teeth into an issue, you weren't likely to shake her. Another one of Mae's trademarks was that of a champion of the underdog. The people in our community knew that if you had an issue with government that they could contact their Senator, Mae Yih, and she would move heaven and earth to help them."

Fred Reed, the plant manager of Willamette Industries' Albany paper mill stated, "Mae has stimulated me to become more involved and more energetic about my beliefs. She has set an incredibly high standard for all of us. There is no halfway with her. She is a person who gives her beliefs one hundred percent."

Gary Grossman, Regional Vice President and Market Manager for Bicoastal Radio wrote, "No meeting was unimportant, no problem was too insignificant for Mae's attention if it was important to one of the people she represented. Many average every-day people have received Mae's attention when they needed her. And when it comes to big legislative matters, Mae has led with her heart and worked incredibly hard for what she sees as good and right. Real public servants only come along once in a while. It has been the good fortune of the people of Linn County and the people of Oregon that Mae came along, and has stayed as long as she has."

Linn County 4-H Leader Roberta Newman wrote, "It always amazed me that as busy as Mae Yih was in her political career, she still felt the calling to volunteer her time for the Shitara exchange program. I know that everyone who worked with her on the annual summer event had the highest regard for her. The Shitara exchange program was so successful because of Mae's attention to detail, her ability to motivate the "troops," and her belief that when people contribute in a positive way, it moves us all closer to world peace."

Finally, Karen Thompson, President of a homecare workers' union, wrote, "I want everyone to know and recognize Senator Mae Yih for her hard work and dedication to the elderly and disabled people of the State of Oregon, especially the ones who depend on the state for their care.

CHAPTER 8: The Campaign Trail

I feel fortunate in the fact that during my entire public service career I never lost an election. The eleven times I put my name before the voters, they responded by electing me. This was in spite of the fact that I began my career in a time when being a middle-aged 49-year-old woman and a minority was seen as a detriment. It was also in spite of the fact that the local media endorsed my opponents in my first several legislative campaigns.

Why was I able to overcome these handicaps and win all my elections? I like to think it is because that beginning from my first election to the school board, I built a track record of hard work and remaining true to my word. Voters knew that I stuck to my principles, that I was honest and frugal, that I fought hard for quality jobs and economic development programs, and that I stood up for the best interests of the people and communities in my district, state and country.

It is also worth mentioning that one of the questions I have been asked numerous times in the course of my political career is whether or not I ever experienced any discrimination because of my Chinese heritage. I suppose that there may have been individuals who voted against me because of my heritage, but given that I never lost an election, any impact was minimal. I never experienced any face-to-face discrimination or racial remarks, but when I first ran for the legislature in 1976, the Corvallis Gazette Times editorialized that I had "a Chinaman's chance of winning." They also said "Mae Yih's chance of winning is like a snowball in July." My attitude is not to make a big deal of it. There is always some degree of discrimination. If you work doubly hard, be persistent, and do what you believe is right, you will prevail in the long run.

I have discussed my school board campaigns and my first campaign for the legislature in 1976 earlier in this book. Here is a brief summary of my other campaigns:

1978: Oregon State House of Representatives: Political professionals will tell you that the best time to beat an incumbent is the first time they run for re-election, so I knew this would be another hard fought campaign. My opponent was a former Albany mayor and developer who did something I always refused to do—run a negative campaign. I believe it is essential that a candidate for public office tells voters what he or she can do, but not what his or her opponent cannot do. My opponent was willing to spend lots of money on his campaign. In fact, the $30,968 he spent was more than any other Oregon state legislative candidate spent that year. My campaign only spent $8,085. As I walked door to door, I was heartened by the kind words of encouragement and support from my constituents. While I was confident of victory on election night, the landslide size of my victory—11,184 votes to 4,990 votes—surprised even me. In other words, he spent almost four times more than I did, but only received less than 30% of the vote. It was proof that honesty, hard work and a "people first" philosophy is the best policy in whatever you do.

1980: Oregon State House of Representatives: This was the easiest of my three House of Representatives campaigns, as no Democrat filed to run against me in the primary, and the Republican candidate was a woman who won her nomination as a write-in, after the one candidate who had filed had her name removed from the ballot when she moved out of the state prior to the primary election. During the campaign, I received my first endorsements from the local Corvallis and Albany newspapers, but my 71%-29% Election Day victory was the most important and satisfying endorsement.

1982: Oregon State Senate: After three terms in the 60-member House of Representatives, I ran for the 30-member Oregon State Senate when John Powell, the Democrat incumbent, decided not to run for re-election. I easily beat a Democrat primary opponent, and my general election Republican opponent was Meredith Wiley, a local attorney and wife of a well-known third generation farmer. She continuously challenged me to five debates. Her campaign strategy assumed she could easily win the election be defeating me in the debates. My answer was that three joint campaign forums had already been agreed to and scheduled, and there wasn't any need for more debates. She continued to send me registered mail demanding more debates, so I finally agreed to one more on the day before the election. In the meantime, I continued canvassing door to door in all 77 precincts of the Senate district, starting from the rural areas, and moving toward city centers as the election drew near. The election night party at our house was a happy one, as I won a 61%-39% victory.

1986: Oregon State Senate: All my 19-hour work days, Saturday morning district office meetings, battling bureaucracies on behalf of my constituents, and common sense approach to keeping taxes low and having the government live within its means paid off when no Republican or Democrat filed to run against me!

1990: Oregon State Senate: When the March 6, 1990 election filing deadline arrived, the only Republican who filed to run against me was a local millworker from Sweet Home. He said the reason he was running was just to give me an opponent, and that he didn't plan to spend more than $500 on his campaign. I didn't take anything for granted, and continued my tradition of canvassing door-to-door. My astute campaign advisor always wanted my campaign events to be more of a fun community get-together rather than about raising money, so my biggest fund raising events were a $5 a plate lamb barbecue and a $5 a plate community spaghetti feed. This was in contrast to legislative fundraisers in other districts, where a ticket price was $100 or even $250. On Election Day in November I received 80% of the vote, and was re-elected by a margin of 23,848-5,978.

1994: Oregon State Senate: My hard work and philosophy of putting the best interests of people first paid off again when I was unopposed for my fourth term in the Oregon State Senate. A Republican candidate had initially filed against me, but shortly before Labor Day, he withdrew his candidacy, saying that he was having marital difficulties. No new Republican candidate indicated interest in taking his place, and on Election Day 1994, I received 28,621 votes—more votes in Linn County than any other candidate for federal, state, or county office.

1998: Oregon State Senate: In what was to be my final campaign, I was elected to my fifth term in the Oregon State Senate by defeating five-term State Representative Carolyn Oakley by a margin of 22,419-13,282. Throughout the campaign, I was heartened by constituents who told me over and over how much they appreciated my hard work. I believe it was that hard work and my goal of accessible representation and achieving accountable and responsible government that people could trust that allowed me to retire from politics never having lost an election.

In each of my elections, I was honored when supporters would take the time to write letters of support to be printed in local community newspapers. There were 67 different letters of support to the editor's mailbag, 23 for the primary election and 44 for the general election. One 1998 letter writer was most enthusiastic when he compared me to England's Princess Diana, who had been killed in 1997 in an automobile accident. I had successfully assisted the writer with a workers' compensation matter. He was injured on the job, had great difficulty in collecting time loss benefits, and was facing imminent foreclosure on his home. I helped him receive his first check within a short time after he contacted me. He wrote that "Senator Yih…is effective with the slightest nudge because she is highly respected and broadly well liked. Diana, Princess of Wales, had similar power…Both the Princess and the Senator are beloved by the people for their deeply felt concern and the benign exercise of their influence. We need more figures of grace like them."

Another 1998 letter writer who was a campground manager for the Sweet Home Ranger District was pleased with my help in getting the Oregon Department of Fish and Wildlife to have 300 hatchery trout released in the Upper South Santiam River. These fish are being stocked for the veterans from the Roseburg VA Hospital. These men were thrilled with the opportunity to fish for the first time in many years. The Sweet Home Veterans Club is hosting a picnic and sponsoring this fishing trip to Yukwah Campground where one of the barrier-free platforms is located. The ODFW said that this is a one-time opportunity and will not set any precedent for future stocking. The campground manager constituent wrote that "Senator Yih has my respect and whole-hearted support in the upcoming election. Mae Yih will devote her energies toward any program that infringes on her constituent's freedoms or rights. She is always out and about the counties discussing real life issues with people, offering her help when needed. Mae doesn't give up. When given a problem, she accepts the challenge, and carries through. She will never back down."

There was also a letter printed in the Albany Democrat Herald from a Lebanon constituent who thanked me for seeing a grievous wrong that needed to be made right. He had received all the necessary DEQ permits to install a well on property he intended to retire on. However, three weeks later, his neighbor drilled a well 70 feet from his drain field. Part of the permit requirement is that no wells could currently exist within 100 feet of his drain field. This was devastating to him. He was now less than the prescribed 100 feet from the neighbor's well with his drain field. He talked to the county and to the water master and was horrified to find that since he had not completed a septic system, they could not correct what his neighbor had done to him. All his pleas to his neighbor, to the county, and to the water master were to no avail.

Finally, he contacted me and I went to work. I discovered that the problem was conflicting bureaucratic rules: the local water master's policy was that his septic system had to be operational before it was deemed to exist, but the DEQ rules stated that it existed from the day it was proposed, thereby meaning his project could go forward. I brought the two agencies together and resolved this bureaucratic double standard that pitted one neighbor against another. This constituent and his wife were able to move into his new home and he expressed his gratitude that I had helped to save him a potential cost of $65,000 and a wrong that had been affecting landowners for many years was made right.

CHAPTER 9: **Five Factors of Political Success**

In the event that one of you might one day run for office—and I hope that you will—- I thought you might be interested in what I believe are the five factors leading to political success. I believe these five factors can be applied to having a successful, well-fulfilled life in other careers, as well.

The first factor is **community involvement**. As I have mentioned several times, it was the advice I received from Barnard College President Millicent McIntosh that inspired me to be involved in school activities when your fathers were attending local grade school. The years I spent as a room mother, a Cub Scout den mother, a hot lunch program coordinator, and PTA vice president and president earned me a reputation for hard work and a deep concern in the quality of our schools. It was that same reputation of hard work and dedication to quality of programs that led to my unintended time in local school boards and Oregon State Legislature. My political career never would have come to pass if I hadn't first been an active community volunteer.

The second factor to succeeding in politics is **trust.** My constituents always said that if you wanted to have anything done, you needed to call Mae Yih. They knew that they could call me any time of the day—early mornings, evenings, weekends or holidays—and they would receive an immediate response. And if my constituents were in the right in fighting for something, they knew they could trust me to be in their corner for as long as it took to resolve the issue satisfactorily. They also knew that, if necessary, I would go to the Governor or to our Congressional delegation to resolve the problem. Over the years, I developed an infamous reputation of being a "bull dog" or even a female "Davey Crockett."

Politicians are famous for making promises they don't keep, thereby losing the trust of their constituents. The only promise I made in all my campaigns was one to be honest, to work hard, and to use common sense. I always remained true to that promise, and, as a result, I never lost the trust of my constituents. One of my common sense approaches is that, just like a family, the government must set priorities, be wise in spending, and live within its means, providing a healthy climate for growth, jobs, and economic development.

The third factor of political success is **personal contact with voters.** My motto in campaigning and in serving was "people first." I would not have won my first election to the legislature, defeating a seven-term incumbent in the process, if I hadn't walked door-to-door, shaking hands, taking notes in my little black book, listening to concerns, and making follow-up responses. That first election taught me a lesson I never forgot. In each of my two additional campaigns for the Oregon House of Representatives and five elections to the Oregon State Senate, I always walked door-to door, and I also walked in community parades—instead of riding in a car, as many politicians did. Even though I won most of these elections by very wide margins, I did not want to take anything for granted. By campaigning door-to-door, by spending Saturday mornings meeting constituents in a local office, by sending proposed legislation to effected citizens at the beginning of each session, by publishing paid bi-weekly or monthly newsletters during the session, and by only introducing legislation that was requested by constituents, I sent a loud and clear message that keeping in close touch with voters and providing prompt follow-up response to their needs was my top priority.

The fourth factor of political success is **financial resources.** The monetary cost of running for office dramatically increased during my public service career. It is also worth noting that most political offices pay salaries much lower than what successful individuals can earn in the private sector. I believe that individuals should not run for political office until they have a sound financial base of their own, so they won't be subject to pressures of campaign contributors. If you are in public service because you need the salary, then you will be tempted to make decisions based on what is best for your re-election, rather than what is best for your constituents. I was very fortunate that your grandfather made a good living as a successful business executive, due to his hard work, sound technical knowledge, and ingenuity. Because of this, I could afford to take important trips to Washington, D.C. and China, entertain visiting dignitaries, and fund five full scholarships for Chinese students to attend graduate school in Oregon. These scholarships reflected my belief that when Chinese students had the opportunity to be educated in Oregon, they would take home with them knowledge of modern technology that would help to improve the quality of life in China, and that they would most likely remember Oregon when trade opportunities arose in the future. These scholarships also enrich friendship, trust, and understanding between the United States and China.

Finally, an important factor of political success is **luck.** When I first ran for the legislature, I was lucky to have politically astute friends who advised me to campaign door-to-door, and I was lucky to have an opponent who took his election for granted. Had I not campaigned door-to-door, and had my opponent worked harder, I might never have served in the legislature. I was also lucky to have a husband who gave me his full support and encouragement in running for office. Your grandfather was a closeted women's libber!

CHAPTER 10: **A Final Thought**

On October 31, 2001, with my last legislative session behind me, I used a speech to the Lebanon Chamber of Commerce to reflect on my life and political career. I made the point that even though I was retiring from politics, I would continue to be involved in the community. I hoped that others would be interested in running for office, even though the pay was low, the workload heavy, complaints and arguments constant, and the sacrifice on the part of family life was enormous. I shared the inspiring words that I first heard as a student from President Millicent McIntosh at Barnard College who challenged us to "use your education, be involved in the decision making process for the benefit of your community." Those words have remained with me throughout my life. They were the words that led me to be involved in school activities, and to run for the school board and the Oregon State Legislature.

So, if you remember anything about this letter from your grandmother, I hope you will remember that I urge you to be involved in your community. Remember that in today's climate, you really cannot afford not to be involved. And remember the many returns that come from serving the public. I was able to meet four U.S. Presidents—John F. Kennedy, Ronald Reagan, George H.W. Bush, Bill Clinton—and five Premiers of China—Deng Xiao Ping, Zhoa Xi Yang, Zue Rong Ji, Jiang Zi Ming, and Wen Ji Pao. I traveled to unique and remote places like Tibet, Xinjiang and Mongolia provinces that I never dreamed I would visit. I had unforgettable experiences like hugging a giant panda and riding a two-hump camel in the desert. Above all, I believe I made a small difference in the quality of life of the constituents I served during my 39 years in public service. My life was enriched and fulfilled at least a hundred times more than if I hadn't been involved in the "decision making process for the benefit of the community." And if you are involved, yours will be, too! As President John Kennedy famously said, "Ask not what your country can do for you; Ask what you can do for your country."

Just as important, I also urge you to remember the core values taught to us by our parents, grandparents, great-grandparents and before: the age old teachings of Confucius being kindness, harmony, character perfection, love of family, the value of lifelong learning, and respect and kindness for others.

CHAPTER 11: **Essay**
Leading and Uniting America in a Time of Change
December, 2012

I applaud the sponsors of the essay contest in calling for discussion on the subject of "Leading and Uniting America in a Time of change." I believe we owe it to our youth to shape and build a bright future for them. We owe it to our forefathers, who have wisely laid a foundation of liberty and free enterprise, and to the men and women before us who have fought hard with supreme sacrifice to preserve our freedom, to maintain America for her leadership position in the world in technology and wealth. Many of my proposed actions are taken from the book "*Free to Choose*" by Nobel Laureate economist Milton Friedman and his wife Rose. Page references in this essay refer to this book. The recommendations might not be politically feasible but they deserve serious consideration.

If I were picked as president tomorrow - in view of the $16 trillion national debt, congressional gridlock, the weak economy, the rapid rise of gas prices, talk of secession, a downgrade of the U.S. debt rating, the looming need for an increase in the debt ceiling, the occupy Wall Street movement and numerous other problems- I would take two immediate steps. First to balance our budget within our income and second to enhance economic opportunities for earning additional revenue to reduce the federal deficit through growth of the economy. The free enterprise system worked well in our nation until the 1928 depression when we started to drift toward expansion of government control and centralization of power, which interferes with and disrupts the market economy.

My highest priority would be to balance the budget within our income. According to a recent news report[1], President Obama has run an annual deficit of approximately $1.7 trillion a year for the last 3 years. He added $5.2 trillion to the national debt; all these deficits have to be financed with borrowed money. It doesn't make sense to continue the borrowing to pay for our programs, it is time to scrutinize our programs,

---

[1] Saunders, Debra, "The Democrats and their no-cut pledge," *Albany Democrat Herald*, December 2, 2012.

examine their cost effectiveness, set priorities, and cut waste and duplication. Due to the congressional gridlock we face, I would urge the governor of each state to introduce and pass legislation to call for a Constitutional amendment to balance the federal budget. Article V of the Constitution provides that the "Congress—on the application of the legislature of two thirds of the several states, shall call a convention for proposing amendments." A movement to call a convention to propose an amendment requiring the federal budget to be balanced was backed by thirty states by mid-1979 (p. 301). This is one device that can effectively bypass the Washington bureaucracy, and given the deadlock in Washington, it seems possible that four more state legislatures would consider calling for such an amendment.

I would also enlist the National Tax Limitation Committee (NTLC) with 250,000 members nationwide to help expedite the process. They can help get the state legislatures to mandate congress to call a national convention to propose an amendment to balance the budget or NTLC can also sponsor a budget balancing amendment for congressional adoption. Appendix B in "Free to Choose" has an example of such an amendment. (p.313)

Because spending for entitlements, especially Social Security, Medicare, and Medicaid, happens automatically, accounts for nearly two thirds of federal spending and is the fastest growing part of the budget[2], we need to examine their cost effectiveness and any alternatives for improvement. Congressional democrats claim that social security is covered through 2033 by its trust fund, but according to OMB, the trust fund's IOU's "do not consist of real economic assets that can be drawn down in the future to fund benefits." "Future benefits will have to be financed by raising taxes, borrowing from the public or reducing benefits or other expenditures."[3] I would suggest doing what the Friedmans proposed as an alternative solution to the social security program (p. 123):

a. Repeal the payroll tax

b. Continue to pay all existing beneficiaries under Social Security the amounts that they are entitled to under current law.

c. Terminate any further accumulation of benefits, allowing individuals to provide for their own retirement as they wish.

d. Finance payment obligations using general tax funds plus the issuance of government bonds.

This transition program does not add in any way to the true debt of the government, it reduces the debt by ending promises to future beneficiaries. It funds what is now unfunded. These steps would enable most of the present social security administrative apparatus to be dismantled at once.(p. 124).

---

[2] Fram, Alan, "How to assess coming debt reduction plan," *Albany Democrat Herald,* November 25, 2012

[3] Krauthammer, Charles, "Why is GOP playing its rivals' game?" *Albany Democrat Herald,* December 2, 2012

The winding down of social security would eliminate its present effect of discouraging employment, which would mean a larger national income. It would add to personal saving and so lead to a higher rate of capital formation and more rapid growth of income. It would stimulate the development and expansion of private pension plans and so add to the security of many workers. (p. 124)
The same solution can be applied to Medicare, similar to Paul Ryan's "premium support" proposal. People should shop for health insurance with government subsidizing purchases by the less affluent. Government would be responsible for its commitment to the existing beneficiaries until the program is phased out.

The Department of Health, Education and Welfare was established in 1953 to consolidate the scattered welfare programs. It began with a budget of $2 billion, less than 5% of the expenditure on national defense. Twenty-five years later in 1978, its budget was $160 billion, one and one-half times as much as total spending on the army, navy and air force. It had the 3rd largest budget in the world, exceeded only by the entire budget of the U.S. government and of the Soviet Union. (p. 96). Today in 2012, thirty four years later, Medicare and Medicaid programs together cost $720 billion a year, about one-fifth of the U.S. budget.[4] Well over 100 federal programs have been enacted to help the poor. (p. 108) Friedmans noted a vast bureaucracy that was largely devoted to shuffling paper rather than to serving people. Once people got on relief, it was hard to get off. Those on relief had little incentive to earn income. While there have been some attempts to reform the welfare system, there is wide spread concern regarding corruption and cheating. The Portland office of DHS is investigating a welfare fraud case involving a couple that has collected housing, welfare, food stamp and other assistance from multiple addresses in the Portland area while living in a five bedroom home in a gated community in Las Vegas[5].

I would recommend Friedman's proposal of a negative income tax as a replacement for the present welfare system, a cash subsidy for those with no other income would be reduced by 50% of income until a break- even point is reached. Beyond that, the regular income taxes would apply. Compared to the existing system, this would give a strong incentive to work. The cost to government would be far less than the cost of the present complex of programs (p. 125). This reform would reduce significantly wasteful spending but would also strengthen families, and provide incentives to work, save and innovate. In Oregon in 1990, there was a fiasco in the state Dept. of Human Resources (DHR) because of their abandonment of a new $14.5 million computer system which the state purchased but couldn't use, despite trying it for a year with help from inside and outside consultants. There was angry outcry regarding the waste of taxpayers' dollars. DHR explained that it purchased the computer to keep track of clients and to

---

[4] Bloomberg News, "Pressure is on for cuts to entitlement programs," *Albany Democrat Herald,* December 7, 2012
[5] Oregon Notes, *The Oregonian* December 11, 2012

prevent welfare fraud, but it turned out that the computer could not track all the complex programs.[6] If the system were as straight forward as the negative income tax provision, it would save a great deal of bureaucracy as well as equipment cost.

On the revenue side, I would try to enhance economic opportunities for earning additional revenues to reduce the federal deficit through growth of the economy:

We can enhance economic opportunities and reduce the federal deficit by cutting the federal agencies' budgets by 40 % or more except for defense and transportation. We have seen enough extravagance of government, high administrative cost, errors and poor performances. Even with all good intentions, the deadening effects of government control are showing in the decline of the economy. Each agency needs to justify its existence, if they prove to limit competition, increase price , lower quality and quantity of products, or eliminate jobs , they need to be reformed or abolished. Licensing agencies need to have a clear published timetable or handbook regarding the application process.

Government expenditures on both older and newer agencies skyrocketed from less than $1 billion in 1970 to roughly $5 billion estimated for 1979. Prices in general roughly doubled but these expenditures more than quintupled. The number of government bureaucrats employed in regulatory activities tripled going from 28,000 in 1970 to 81,000 in 1979. During the same decade economic growth in the U.S. slowed drastically from 1949-1969. Output per man-hour of all persons employed in private business rose more than 3% a year, in the next decade less than half as fast and by the end of the decade productivity was actually declining. (p. 190, MF.) Whatever the announced objectives, all of the movements in government regulation have been anti-growth. They have been opposed to new developments, to industrial innovation, to the increased use of natural resources. Agencies have imposed heavy costs on industry after industry to meet increasingly detailed and extensive government requirements. They have prevented products from being produced or sold, required capital to be invested for nonproductive purposes in ways specified by government and bureaucrats. OSHA is a prime example- a bureaucratic nightmare that has produced an outpouring of complaints. As one joke has it. How many Americans does it take to screw in a light bulb? Answer: Five; one to screw in the bulb, four to fill out the environmental impact and OSHA reports. (p.243). Another example: Edward Teller, the great nuclear physicist, once put it" It took 18 months to build the first nuclear power generator; it now takes twelve years; that's progress." The money spent by the government is causing costs to industry and consumer of complying with the regulations. (Conservative estimates put the cost at something like $100 billion a year,) and that doesn't count the cost to the consumer of restricted choice and higher prices for the products that are available.

---

[6] Obert, Gail "Computer fiasco to bring grilling" *Albany Democrat Herald* July 21, 1990 p.3

A recent example of bureaucracy shows up in a news article.[7] Aquabounty of Maynard, Mass, which produced a genetically modified salmon that grows twice as fast as normal fish, could not get FDA's approval for marketing the fish after working with the FDA since 1993. In 2010 the FDA concluded that Aquabounty's salmon was as safe to eat as the traditional variety and there's little chance that the salmon could escape and breed with wild fish. Almost twenty years of working with the FDA, the FDA has not approved the fish and Aquabounty is running out of money. The company has burned through more than $67 million since it started. Aquabounty had only enough money to survive until January 2013. The unexplained delay in FDA's approval has made raising money for the company difficult. FDA says it's still working on the final piece of its review, a report on the potential environmental impact of the salmon that must be published for comments before an approval can be issued. That means a final decision could be months even years away. The delay could mean that the faster growing salmon will never wind up on American dinner tables. Scientists worry that its experience with the FDA's lengthy review process could discourage other U.S. companies from investing in animal biotechnology or the science of manipulating animal DNA to produce a desirable trait. That would put the U.S. at a disadvantage at a time when China, India and other foreign governments are pouring millions of dollars each year into the potentially lucrative field that could help reduce food costs and improve food safety.

Researchers at the UC Davis have transferred an experimental herd of genetically engineered goats that produce protein rich milk to Brazil due to concern about delays at the FDA, and Canadian researchers pulled their FDA application for a biotech pig that would produce environmentally friendly waste.

The story of Aquabounty is disappointing said Professor Helen Sang, a geneticist at the University of Edinburgh in Scotland, who is working to develop genetically modified chickens that are resistant to bird flu. "Because it's gotten so bogged down- and presumably cost AquaBounty a huge amount of money- I think people will be put off."

Another example of the Washington agencies that have placed no interest in the welfare of people they are purported to serve is the cut back of logging for the protection of the spotted owl. In 1990 when the spotted owl, salmon and ants are recommended for listing in the endangered species act, the U.S. Fish and Wildlife Dept. wanted to set aside 3 million acres, approximately the size of the state of Connecticut for the owls' critical habitat. Timber industry, workers, state and elected officials warned that 28,000 jobs would be lost in the next decade;[8] Oregon should be allowed to manage its own resources responsibly for protection of the owl as well as for industry and jobs.

---

[7] Perrone, Matthew, "Fast-growing salmon may not wind up on your plate," *Albany Democrat Herald,* December 5, 2012

[8] Sonner,Scott "Spotted owl listed as threatened" Albany Democrat Herald June22, 1990

Now, twenty five years later, we have a 90% cut back in logging, Oregon has one of the highest unemployment rates in the nation, a recent news report,[9] U.S. Fish and Wildlife came back and wanted another 9.6 million acres of Oregon, Washington and NW California land to be dedicated to protecting the spotted owl because the spotted owl has seen a 40% decline.[10] No mention was made about any efforts to control the invasion of the barred owl an east coast cousin that has been pushing the meeker spotted owl out of its territories and the fact that spotted owl was known to survive in the second and third growth forests in California. Federal agencies' excessive regulatory control has taken away Oregon workers' jobs, their freedom to make a living, the timber industry's opportunity to operate their mills and led to consumers paying higher price for wood products. Government also have to pay extra costs in unemployment benefits, job training, counseling, dislocated workers funds, welfare and numerous other programs when they are forced out of their jobs.

Another example of a government agency's excessive regulations that threatens jobs, increases costs to businesses and prevents future investment, happened also in 1990. The state Department of Environmental Quality (DEQ) under the guidelines of the federal Environmental Protection Agency (EPA) required the paper mills in Oregon to limit dioxin discharge due to their pulp bleaching process to .013 parts dioxin to quadrillion parts water, the same proportion as 1 second in 2 billion years due to their concerns regarding human health. The discharge requirement was not backed by science data nor is it measurable or achievable by available technology yet violation means a penalty of $10,000 a day effective 1992. 700 jobs are at stake at the Halsey pulp mill, it also meant a delay or cancelling of a $400 million planned expansion. In January 1990 DEQ reduced the discharge permit level to .2 mg per day from the current level of .68 mg daily which is down 60% from 1.6mg in 1988. In August, DEQ further proposed tightening it to .14 mg per day as an annual average. The pulp mill appealed the limit as too restrictive; the DEQ's proposed limits could stop the pulp and paper industry in Oregon and cancel plans for growth. The mill officials decided it could reduce the limit to .3 mg per day level by retrofitting the existing mill at a cost of about $50 million. A common size aspirin tablet is 250 mg. State DEQ was asked if they have data to prove that such a restrictive limit is justified, their answer was that their mission was not to do research but to enforce regulation under EPA guidelines.

A Willamette River study was initiated by the Oregon Legislative Emergency Board at my request in March, 1990 funded jointly by the state, pulp industry and municipalities to analyze the pollutants in the river, their sources and whether they are at levels

---

[9] Barnard,Jeff, "Feds aim to double spotted owl habitat" Albany Democrat Herald, Nov. 22, 2012

[10] O'Connor, Patio H&N Political Writer "Owl at least a start" Harald & News, Klamath Falls, Oregon April 22, 1990

that are harmful to humans. According to the preliminary results of the Oregon State University OSU study of the Willamette River in January 1991, measurable dioxin contamination has been found in some fish virtually throughout the Willamette River system. The amounts of dioxin accumulation were above levels outlined by the U.S. EPA as a concern for consumption of contaminated fish. But they are 25 times lower than levels specified by the U.S. Food and Drug Administration for restricting fisheries. Preliminary results of the 3-yr study of the Willamette River found the same concentration of dioxin about 1 part per trillion at 5 sampling sites of the Willamette river. Two above the Halsey mill and two below. The same 1 part per trillion concentrations up and down the river from Halsey showed that the pulp mill was not a major point source for dioxin and the river was able to take care of dioxin in it. Other sources of dioxin are use of wood preservatives, herbicide, municipal incineration of plastics and the manufacture of pulp and paper.

At one part per trillion, the dioxin level found in squaw fish were 14 times higher than the level the EPA has specified as a concern for consumption of such fish. The EPA threshold for concern was set at 0.07 parts per trillion.[11] However, levels of 25 parts per trillion are allowed under the U.S. FDA before fisheries are curtailed. Canada has an advisory level of 20 parts per trillion.[12]

U.S. Food and Drug Administration (FDA) and state health officers not EPA issue fish advisories. This shows regulatory agencies making excessive demands on industries without thorough scientific studies and coordination with each other causing huge costs to businesses and threatens productivity, well-paid jobs, capital investments and expansions.

Energy Independence: We import approximately 62% of our petroleum, amounting to U.S. spending a billion dollars a day on imported oil. This has created a tremendous trade deficit, affected our national defense, drove up the price of gas and weakened our economy and national security. U.S. Admiral Hyman Rickover, the father of the U.S. navy nuclear submarine fleet under President Carter's administration urged for individual sacrifices for the common good in building energy independence and said "the energy challenge should be considered the moral equivalent of war- except that we will be uniting our efforts to build- not to destroy."[13] Transportation *consumes* 77% of the total petroleum used in the U.S., we can make real progress by conservation, renovation and research. I would encourage more use of electric and natural gas cars, build more nuclear energy generating plants while doing further research in cost effective alterna-

---

[11] OSU News Service "Study shows traces pf dioxin widespread in Willamette River "Albany Democrat Herald Jan. 11, 1991 p.3

[12] Jameson, Hunter "Consultant pleased with study" Albany Democrat Herald, Jan. 11, 1991 p.3

[13] Hakes, Jay "A Declaration of Energy Independence" John Wiley & Sons, Inc. p.46

tive energy and "advanced generation reactors including the use of high temperature gas cooled reactors to generate hydrogen for transportation needs."[14]

Free Trade: We, as the leader of the free world, can declare that we offer free trade and free cooperation on equal terms to all. Our market is open without tariffs or other restrictions. Nations can sell us what they can and wish to, buy whatever they can and wish to. In that way cooperation among individuals and businesses can be worldwide and free. (p.50)

The need to meet foreign competition rather than being sheltered behind government barriers might very well produce a stronger and more efficient industry than we have today. (p.46)

International free trade fosters harmonious relations among nations that differ in culture and institutions, just as free trade at home fosters harmonious relations among individuals who differ in beliefs, attitudes, and interests.

We can achieve free trade through a constitutional amendment to say "Congress shall not lay any imposts or duties on imports or exports except what may be absolutely necessary for executing its inspection laws." (p 304) The attack on all tariffs consolidates the interests we all have as consumers to counter the special interests we each have as producers. (p.304)

As China with its 1.4 billion populations improves its standard of living we have a huge potential market in its growing middle class in consumer goods and capital investments.

Defense: The defense budget would not face a 40% cut, but it needs to scale down as war is winding down. We need an adequate defense budget, but we don't need to be policeman of the world. We need to respect the sovereignty of each nation and cultural differences while working towards common goals of peace and cooperation.

Transportation: The budget would not face a 40% cut, but gas tax revenue needs to be dedicated entirely to the building and maintenance of roads and bridges, not to be borrowed or used in other programs.

Taxes: An essential part of economic freedom is freedom to choose how to use our income, how much to spend, save and how much to give away. Currently more than 40 % of our income is disposed of on our behalf by government at federal, state and local levels combined.

I would promote a constitutional amendment to give the government a limited budget, specified in advance, the way each of us has a limited budget. (p.303).This was also discussed previously.

---

[14] Graham, Ron "Making a Case for Nuclear Energy" ATI Wah Chang Outlook Second & Third Quarter 2008 p. 20

Income tax : After the federal budget is balanced, an amendment to the 6th Constitutional Amendment can be recommended to allow a low flat rate income tax- less than 20% - on all income above personal exemptions with no deductions except for strict occupational expenses. This would yield more revenue than the present unwieldy structure. (p.306)

Any difference between an increase in revenue and government outlay can be used to reduce the federal debt.

Corporate income tax: This should be abolished. It constitutes double taxation of corporate income –once to the corporation and once to the stock holder when the income is distributed. It penalizes capital investment and thereby hinders growth in productivity. (p. 306)

Repeal of payroll tax: This was discussed previously under social security reform.

Public Schools: I support the move to a voucher system recommended by Friedman so that parents can have more control. Centralization and bureaucratization of schools have increased drastically professional staff and cost while decreasing the quality of education as evidenced by declining grades recorded on standardized examination. (p. 156). We need to give parents greater freedom of choice as they have more interest and intimate knowledge of their children's capacities and needs. Issuing vouchers to parents would reduce the duplication of cost to them while allowing more competition in the school system to enhance quality and reduce cost.

University: Based on two detailed studies, one for Florida and one for California, (p.182), government financing of higher education is inequitable in its effects. The middle and upper income classes have benefited from the poor subsidizing higher education due to more students from the mid to upper income groups pursuing higher education. The top income class got a net gain; it got back 60% more than it paid. The bottom two classes paid 40 % more than they got back, the middle class paid nearly 20% more.(p.182). In so far as government operates higher education, universities should charge students fees corresponding to the full cost of the educational and other services they provide. There is a strong case for government providing loan funds sufficient to ensure opportunity to all, provided the student is willing to pay for it either currently or out of the higher income the schooling will enable him or her to earn. (p.183)

In addition to the economic reforms mentioned above, I would recommend that schools teach values, family and personal virtue, achieve character perfection in discipline, high integrity, love and respect within the family, community, nation and the world.

Acknowledgements

A special thanks to my long-time friend Kerry Tymchuk, the Executive Director of the Oregon Historical Society, who provided wise counsel and assistance in making this book a reality.